CELEBRATION OF HAND-HOOKED RUGS XXII
2012 Edition

Editor
Debra Smith

Author
Ayleen Stellhorn

Designer
CW Design Solutions, Inc.

Circulation/Advertising Coordinator
Gail Weaverling

Magazine Assistants
Candice R. Derr
Kathryn Fulton

Operations Manager
Anne Lodge

Publisher
Judith Schnell

Rug photographs provided by the artist unless otherwise noted.

Rug Hooking magazine is published five times a year in Jan./Feb., March/April/May, June/July/Aug., Sept./Oct., and Nov./Dec. by Stackpole, Inc., 5067 Ritter Road, Mechanicsburg, PA 17055. *Celebration of Hand-Hooked Rugs* is published annually. Contents Copyright© 2012. All rights reserved. Reproduction in whole or part without the written consent of the publisher is prohibited. Canadian GST #R137954772.

NOTICE: All patterns and hooked pieces presented here are Copyright© the individual designers, who are named in the corresponding captions. No hooked piece presented here may be duplicated in any form without the designer's consent.

A Publication of
RUG HOOKING

5067 Ritter Road
Mechanicsburg, PA 17055
(717) 796-0411
(877) 462-2604
www.rughookingmagazine.com
rughook@stackpolebooks.com

ISBN-978-1-881982-85-2

Printed in U.S.A.

Welcome Celebration XXII

We are proud to present the newest edition of *Rug Hooking* magazine's *Celebration* series. This year's rugs are as exciting as ever and you'll find that *Celebration XXII* is full to the brim of exquisite rugs of all styles. Realistic, stylistic, impressionistic, abstract; traditional, primitive, portraits, landscapes: you will find incredible hooked pieces to inspire and amaze you.

Each year it seems that more and more original rugs are entered, and this year was no exception. What a great commentary on the state of our craft: rug hookers are embracing the opportunity to conceive and design their own unique pieces. You will be charmed by the wide range of fantastic and imaginative creations.

This year we received many more entries from Texas and California than from any other location. Certainly state size and population contribute to larger numbers, but it does appear that something more may be going on here. Is rug hooking growing in the Southwest and on the West Coast? We'll have to wait and see what next year brings before we call it a trend; it is wonderful to have rugs in *Celebration* from all over the continent and beyond: from Nova Scotia and Prince Edward Island to California, from British Columbia and Alberta to Georgia.

Enjoy this collection of incredible hooked rugs. They are now part of the *Celebration* legacy, celebrated throughout the textile world as some of the finest rugs ever hooked. Settle back and get ready for the show!

Readers' Choice
Remember to be a part of the Readers' Choice decision: vote for your favorite hooked rugs! You can vote either with the paper ballot included in this book, or digitally. Go to **www.rughookingmagazine.com,** and look for **Celebration Readers' Choice Voting**. Or use the enclosed ballot and return it to us by mail. We must have your vote by **December 31, 2012.**

On the Cover: *Fantasy Flight, Lyle Drier. Read more about her rug on pages 20–21.*

Table of Contents

page 90

Welcome to *Celebration XXII* 1
Meet the Judges 4

RUGS BASED ON ORIGINAL DESIGNS 7

African Dreams 8
Sharon Stapleton, Tualatin, Oregon

Aries Woman 10
Mariah Krauss, Montpelier, Vermont

Caryn's Passion 12
Caryn Linn, Eau Claire, Wisconsin

Chocolate Chip 14
Carol Kassera, Aledo, Texas

Crow 16
Kaye D. Miller, Louisville, Kentucky

Delightful Friends 18
Cec Caswell, Sherwood Park, Alberta, Canada

Fantasy Flight 20
Lyle Drier, Waukesha, Wisconsin

Geronimo 22
Grace Collette, Raymond, New Hampshire

Hellebores 24
Kerri Kolbe, Bolton, Connecticut

Kristen in the Adirondacks 26
Anne Bond, Northville, Michigan

Mr. "GQ" 28
Judith Rippstein, Fredericksburg, Texas

My Happy Captain in Metz 30
Sunny Runnells, Lantzville, British Columbia, Canada

Noah's Ark Sampler 32
Susan Quicksall, Oglesby, Texas

Patrick and Logan at Balsam Lake: Summer of 2009 34
Trish Johnson, Toronto, Ontario, Canada

Pennsylvania 36
Jan Winter, Hollywood, California

Remembering Spring 38
Cheryl Bollenbach, Golden, Colorado

Sorrow 40
Ivi Nelson Collier, Nottingham, Maryland

Still Life #8—The Bowl of Onions 42
Carol Koerner, Bethesda, Maryland

Summer Winds 44
Bea Brock, Kerrville, Texas

Swamp Critters 46
Corrine Watts, Washington, DC

The Grand Canyon 48
Mary Jo Lahners, Lincoln, Nebraska

Toolbox 50
Anne-Marie Littenberg, Burlington, Vermont

Wedding Dance 52
Eric Sandberg, Athens, Georgia

With Closed Eyes 54
Judy Cole, Shelburne, Vermont

RUGS BASED ON COMMERCIAL DESIGNS 57

8-Cut Rose 58
Ellen M. Jensen, Martinsburg, Pennsylvania

American Kestrel 60
Sheila Mitchell, Victoria, British Columbia, Canada

Anatolian 62
Jeanne Benjamin, Brookfield, Massachusetts

Cape Shore Crewel 64
Fran Oken, Rutland, Vermont

Daghestan Prayer Rug 66
Cathy Williams, Los Gatos, California

Eden's Floor 68
Carol Lynn Gillingham, Helotes, Texas

For Your Love 70
Connie Bradley, Wellington, Ohio

Grenfell Goose 72
Leslie Cuthbertson, Airdrie, Alberta, Canada

Jumbo Star 74
Janet Griffith, Frisco, Texas

Leaf Border Geometric 76
Linda Gustafson, Chardon, Ohio

Pemaquid Lighthouse 78
Ellen Forstrom, North Haledon, New Jersey

Rugs by the Sea 80
Jo Ann Hendrix, Pasadena, Maryland

Victorian Garden 82
Judy Colley, Wyoming, Michigan

RUGS BASED ON ADAPTATIONS 85

Bonneville 200 MPH Club Life Member 86
Betty Magan, Bass Lake, California

Dad 88
Cindy Irwin, Pequea, Pennsylvania

Gold Hill, UK 90
Bernice Howell, Beltsville, Maryland

Hawa 92
Jackie Roop, Charlottetown, Prince Edward Island, Canada

Indian Boy—Ah-Chee-Lo 94
Donna K. Hrkman, Dayton, Ohio

La Japonaise 96
Karen Whidden, Southern Pines, North Carolina

Lake Shore 98
Roland C. Nunn, Orinda, California

Ram Tough 100
Michele Wise, Seabeck, Washington

Southern Leopard Frog and Tri-colored Heron 102
Judy Carter, Willow Street, Pennsylvania

Sylvia 104
Kay Bowman, New Glasgow, Nova Scotia, Canada

The Beauty of Keith Richards 106
Mischelle Page Hodgkin, Winchester, Kentucky

Turtle Reflection 108
Jon Ciemiewicz, Hudson, New Hampshire

RUGS BASED ON PRIMITIVE DESIGNS . . .111

Animal Crackers 112
Gail Ferdinando, Pittstown, New Jersey

Distelfink 114
Cynthia Norwood, Austin, Texas

Four and Twenty Blackbirds 116
Wendy Powell, Santa Ynez, California

Yankee Ingenuity 118
Teresa Heinze, Lubbock, Texas

HONORABLE MENTIONS 121

Couldn't a Fire Outrun a Galloping Horse? 122
Halina Bienkowski, Amherst, Nova Scotia, Canada

Flight 122
Liz Marino, South Egremont, Massachusetts

Sable Island Horse No. 1 .122
Suzanne Gunn, Centreville, Nova Scotia, Canada

Alamo Garden 123
Phyllis Mulligan, Swannanoa, North Carolina

Beauty and the Beast 123
Katy Powell, Portland, Oregon

My Labs 123
Chizuko Hayami, Setagaya, Tokyo, Japan

Palazzo Di Piero 124
Janet T. Conner, Hiram, Maine

Somewhere Over the Bakken (in the Badlands of ND) . . .124
Carolyn Godfread, Bismark, North Dakota

Halloween Hooligans 124
Natasha Chan, Carmel, Indiana

Seasons of the Heart 126
Joan Sample, Woodinville, Washington

Midnight Clear 126
Kris Miller, Howell, Michigan

Tuhay 126
Marion Sachs, York, Pennsylvania

CELEBRATING PRIMITIVE DESIGN 129

Antique Heart in Hand Redux 129
Norma Batastini, Glen Ridge, New Jersey

Elaine's Antique Runner .130
Debra Inglis, San Augustine, Texas

Unbridled 130
Susan Higgins, San Francisco, California

Oliver Cromwell 131
Cora Maldonado, Texas City, Texas

Peace, Love and Dan 132
Laurie Wiles, Edmonton, Alberta, Canada

Shippee Floral 134
Weslee Hursh, Brownsville, Pennsylvania

Newfoundland Lion 134
Pam Upton, Lake Crystal, Minnesota

Remember 136
Georgeanne Wertheim, San Antonio, Texas

Shenandoah Valley Eagle 136
Crystal Brown, Washington, Pennsylvania

Meet the Judges

Each year a new panel of judges takes on the daunting task of evaluating *Celebration* entries. Imagine the enormity of the task: each entry comes with 4 separate photos, so in a field of 200 entries the judges will review and evaluate a total of 800 photographs. With our current system of online judging, the process is more judge-friendly than in the days when they traveled here to view the entries, one slide at a time. But consider the task that they face: even sitting in their own homes in a favorite chair with a cup of coffee nearby, it is an enormous commitment of time and energy. Hours and hours of concentration, deliberation, and careful consideration; the judges essentially commit one week in early January to *Celebration* judging. All for the love of rug hooking.

We are so pleased that each year we have people willing to act as judges. It is their expertise and wide-ranging experience that makes *Celebration* work so well; they are the foundation of the whole enterprise.

And so we extend our heartfelt thanks to these four women and to all the judges who have gone before them. And, please . . . if you have an opportunity, be sure to thank a judge. Their contributions cannot be overstated.

Anita White
Overland Park, Kansas

Anita started rug hooking in 1994 while living in Alaska. As an antique dealer, she had bought and sold several antique rugs. She decided to try her hand at hooking her own rugs, so she started with a small rug from a kit, then hooked three more small mats. When Anita moved to Kansas she began taking classes and she attended many workshops.

Anita is a McGown certified teacher, teaching at her home in Overland Park since 1997 and at many camps and workshops around the country since 2000. She inspires and encourages students from beginners to seasoned hookers. She is best known for her textured wide-cut style and use of antique paisley. Many of her happiest days are spent with a dye pot, creating wonderful wools to use in her work and her classes.

Anita's work has appeared in *RHM* and *Early American Life*. She is a member of ATHA and the State Line Rug Hookers Guild. In her free time, Anita likes to antique, camp, fish, and run.

Anne Boissinot
Toronto, Ontario

Anne has been a Certified Canadian and McGown teacher for over 40 years. She is past president of the Ontario Hooking Craft Teachers Branch and past education program chair for the Ontario Teachers Branch. She has played a variety of roles in this organization to further the art of teaching and the development of teaching practices.

She served as past president of the Southern McGown Teachers Workshop and past vice president of the National Pearl K. McGown Guild. She is a member of ATHA, TIGHR, the Nova Scotia Guild, the Western Canada Guild, and the OHCG.

Anne studied art history and art and related courses at Sheridan College. She has been a judge and juror for OHCG craft shows and fairs.

Anne currently teaches design, color, and dyeing. Her published articles appear in *RHM*, the Ontario Hooking Craft Guild and Ontario Teachers Newsletters, and the McGown newsletter. She volunteered with the Mexican Rug Hooking Group in San Miguel in 2010.

Vivily Powers
Manchester, Connecticut

Vivily started hooking in 1967 at an adult evening school class with Maggie McClea after a family friend showed her some hooked crewel designs. Vivily soon realized that hooking—especially crewel designs—had become a passion. In addition to basic rug hooking techniques, Maggie taught Vivily how to dye, embellish, and to work with all cuts and designs. Vivily eventually took over adult evening classes and started teaching day classes at the Fraser rug studio where she developed a long relationship with Bob and Jeanette Sztkowski. Vivily expanded her knowledge of dyeing and color with Maryanne Lincoln and Sally Newhall.

Vivily has a background in textiles and taught home economics. She is a member of the McGown, ATHA, and Nova Scotia guilds. She is the past president and chairman of education for the McGown guild and has had the honor of being the director of a national exhibit.

As a McGown certified teacher, Vivily continues her education by attending and teaching at several teacher workshops annually, as well as participating in national, local, and museum exhibits.

In the early 1980s, Vivily's love of textiles, color, and dyeing led her to purchase the Colorama line of swatches. Vivily has continued and expanded the line over the years.

Kathleen Harwood
Montrose, Pennsylvania

Kathleen is an art historian and appraiser, dealer, author, and lecturer whose career has encompassed many aspects of the art world, including 16 years as an appraiser of fine art on PBS's *Antiques Roadshow*. She is also a passionate textile artist. For the last 10 years she has focused on hooked rugs, which she designs and hooks with an eye to historical sources interpreted in colorful, contemporary ways. Her rugs were selected for *Celebration XX* and *XXI*. She has organized gallery exhibitions of hooked rugs, and she teaches. Kathleen lives with her husband and two dogs on a lake in rural Pennsylvania where she gardens madly and tries hard to contribute to the quality of life in her community.

Sauder Village
2012 Rug Hooking Week

Exhibit & Vendors, August 15 - 18... Our extensive exhibit includes the Main Exhibit, Annual Theme Challenge *"Olympic Grandeur," "Eye See You II"* and *"Zodiac Collection"* Special Exhibits and Rug Hooking Magazine's *Celebration XXII* Exhibit. Leading vendors in the rug hooking industry will have a vast selection of items for your shopping enjoyment.

Retreats, August 14 - 17... Three and Four Day Retreats with teachers Barbara Carroll (PA), Judy Carter (PA), Beverly Conway (VT), Donna Hrkman (OH), Trish Johnson (Canada) and Linda Pietz (CA).

Workshops, August 15 - 18... Half and full day workshops from Wednesday - Saturday taught by creative and talented retreat and special guest teachers. More details are available on our website at: www.saudervillage.org/Creativity/rughooking.asp.

Join us in 2013!
August 14-17, 2013
Rug Hooking Week at Sauder Village

Details available on our website this fall!

In Northwest Ohio! • 22611 St. Rt. 2, Archbold, OH 43502 • 800.590.9755 • www.SauderVillage.org

Searsport Rug Hooking

A great selection "Maine-made" hooks & frames, kits, dyes, frasier, & bliss cutters; 100's of hand-drawn primitive patterns on the straight of the grain. Over 1,000 yards of bolt wool and over-dyed wool in stock!

NEW 102 inch wide Linen!
In Stock — Call today to order.

Hookin' the sunshine state!
Hookin' in Sarasotta — February 2013

Hookin' the high seas!
Rug Hooking Cruise — February 2013
Call for more information.

Are you In the Loop?
Sign-up online for our digital newsletter, In the Loop, to stay abreast of our hookin' events and specials!

207-249-0891
www.searsportrughooking.com
11 West Side Drive, Verona Island, ME 04416
10 a.m. through 5 p.m. ♦ Closed Tuesdays

SHOWCASE OF
Original Designs

A work composed firsthand

Merriam Webster's Collegiate Dictionary, 11th edition

ORIGINAL

An original rug is designed and hooked from an original idea with original content and interpretation.

Celebration XXII 2012 • 7

ORIGINAL DESIGNS

African Dreams

Sharon Stapleton designed this rug for her parents' 50th wedding anniversary. She found herself mesmerized by the pictures of the Maasai people, their war shields, and their expressive art. "They use certain colors in their designs as they are limited by the pigments provided by nature," she says. "On the other hand, the peoples of Africa are surrounded by animals and birds that are extremely vibrant. It is amazing how each animal has unique stripes, spots, and coloration, but then adapts to blend into the landscape."

When she is ready to design and color plan a rug, Sharon retires to what she calls her "wool room" and surrounds herself with an expanse of colors and textures. Only then can she begin the creative process. For *African Dreams*, she decided to incorporate the African spear, the Maasai colors, and geometric motifs.

Sharon hooked wool off the bolt as well as spot-dyed, over-dyed, and dip-dyed wools created by Shelley Flannery and Barbara Hanson.

The lion is her favorite part of the finished rug because of the strength and resilience he embodies. However, it was also the most challenging part to complete. "Thumbing through a quilting magazine, I noticed how the artist was able to create realistic faces using 'segments of color' rather than fine lines or an expanse of different shades of the same color," she says. "I experimented with hooking sections of lion faces using this technique as a guide. After hooking two prior lions, I liked how this one turned out."

Sharon finished her rug with textured knitting wool. The fuzzy earth-colored wool that she chose fit the theme of the rug not just in coloration, but also in style.

In the Judges' Words

- Dramatic and original.
- Nice depiction of African animals in their natural habitat.
- Good color balance and design.

Sharon Stapleton
Tualatin, Oregon

A brain-injury from an accident in 2005 left Sharon unable to continue her job as a pediatric critical care flight nurse. She discovered rug hooking as a way to boost her concentration and strengthen her right hand in an effort to calm the tremors she still experiences. She has completed 35 rugs in almost 6 years. Sharon currently volunteers at a therapeutic horse-riding facility. Her rugs have received blue ribbons at state fairs; this is her first appearance in Celebration.

8 • Celebration XXII 2012

African Dreams, 32" x 39", #4- and 5-cut hand-dyed and bolt wool on monk's cloth. Designed and hooked by Sharon Stapleton, Tualatin, Oregon, 2011. ANNA LANCASTER

ORIGINAL DESIGNS

Aries Woman

Mariah Krauss likes detail, finely shaded swatches with 15-plus values, and contemporary themes. "I try to make every piece convey an emotion that catches the viewer and doesn't let go; I want people to feel what I felt when creating each piece."

The creative spark for *Aries Woman* came from a very specific feeling, and Mariah wanted to stay true to that feeling as she worked on this rug from beginning to end. "It was meant to display all aspects of my personality," she says. "She is wild, dangerous, thoughtful, guarded, beautiful, overwhelming, occasionally out of control, and still has so much to learn. She is Aries, the goddess."

Mariah color planned the rug based on a 30-value swatch she dyed. Dyeing that swatch took three weeks. She dyed the new white wool in a pot on the stove, energetically stirring each piece of wool until the water was clear so she would have colored pieces that were as solid and unvaried as possible.

In all, Mariah needed about a year and a half to complete the rug: planning the rug took about two months, creating the pattern took another three months, and hooking and framing took about a year. She found that the most difficult part of completing the rug was creating the pattern and honing the idea.

She finished the rug with a black wool binding over stretcher bars, and the completed rug currently hangs in her mother's shop. Her favorite aspect of the finished rug is the feedback she has received from friends and strangers about the emotions the rug conjures. "I created it to share," she says, "and I'm thrilled that so many people want to share it with me."

In the Judges' Words

- Unbelievable control of color and value.
- Artistically magnificent!
- Impressed by the shading of the face as it recedes into the background.
- LOVE that wild hair.

Mariah Krauss
Montpelier, Vermont

Mariah is a fifth generation rug hooker whose grandmother started Green Mountain Rug School in 1982. She has been around rug hooking her whole life and "through osmosis has soaked up quite a bit of knowledge." She has been hooking seriously for the past two years, and Aries Woman is her fifth rug. It won awards at the Shelburne Show in 2011 and marks her first appearance in Celebration.

Aries Woman, 26" x 18", #2-, 3-, and 4-cut wool strips on monk's cloth.
Designed and hooked by Mariah Krauss, Montpelier, Vermont, 2011.

ORIGINAL DESIGNS

Caryn's Passion

In the Judges' Words

- Nicely done self-portrait.
- Facial features are nicely executed through the use of color.
- The colors are fabulous, interesting, and subtle at the same time.
- I like the way the figure overlaps the edges of the picture plane and blends into the distance.

A class with Sharon Townsend on hooking faces encouraged Caryn Linn to focus not on someone else's face, but on her own. "I thought this was the perfect opportunity to do a piece of my young daughters; however, Sharon thought it was best to start with a self-portrait."

To get started, Caryn asked her husband to take photos of her from several different angles as she was hooking. From all the choices, she chose this one.

Color planning for the rug actually began with the photo shoot. Caryn thought about the colors she wanted to hook then dressed in clothing that matched her choices. Her choice of furniture and pose were also planned in advance, as well as which piece of hooked art she would be holding in her lap. Caryn dyed all new wool for the project in a crock pot.

From several photos, she chose one and enlarged it at a local photography shop. She then transferred the outlines to Red Dot and then to linen. She was careful to get the transferred lines just right from the beginning so her project would be off to a solid start.

Caryn worked on the rug on and off for about nine months until she met Tish Murphy at a rug camp where she learned the details to really complete the piece. Her favorite parts of the finished rug are the hand and the face. This was also the most difficult part to hook because of the challenges she faced in using primitive shading. However, by using lights and darks and values in between, Caryn successfully captured the three-dimensional facial features and the curve of her hand.

Caryn Linn
Eau Claire, Wisconsin

Caryn started taking classes with Mary Ellen Keller after seeing a hooked piece in a friend's home. In the 15 years since then she has hooked 20 rugs, including a 5-foot by 7-foot primitive, plus many purses, pillows, and mats. She regularly attends camps and is a member of the Chippewa Valley Rug Hookers. Her selection for inclusion in Celebration *is her first rug hooking award.*

Caryn's Passion, 29" x 26½", #4-, 6- and 8-cut wool on linen.
Designed and hooked by Caryn Linn, Eau Claire, Wisconsin, 2010.

ORIGINAL DESIGNS

Chocolate Chip

When Carol Kassera finished this rug she told her husband she would never frame anything this big again. Ever. Compared to that chore, hooking *Chocolate Chip* was a breeze.

Carol's inspiration for this design came from the herd of longhorn cattle that parade down Main Street in Fort Worth, Texas, to their grazing pastures then parade back up Main Street at the end of the day. The city's motto is "Where the West begins," and the longhorn steer is a well-known symbol of the Old West.

The animal she chose to be the central figure of the rug is named Chocolate Chip. Carol decided to use Chocolate Chip's likeness because of his unusual coloring. While color planning the rug, she decided on a colorful, natural background that wouldn't compete with the mostly white animal. She also decided to hook him vertically to make him stand apart even more. She color planned the sky so the clouds would reflect the purples in the field.

Carol found the wool that she needed for Chocolate Chip, the flowers at his feet, and the landscape behind him in her bag of scraps. She dyed wool for the sky and the clouds, using swatches, spot dyes, and dip dyes.

Her biggest challenge in hooking the rug was the clouds. "It is difficult to hook them to make them look natural," she says, "not like they are pasted on."

When she was done hooking the rug she had a frame custom made and glued leather inserts in to form a background that would directly relate to the rug. Her favorite part of the finished piece is Chocolate Chip himself. "He hooked up exactly like what I had in mind," she says.

In the Judges' Words

- Good contrast of cow against the peaceful background.
- Good design exhibiting good color and depth.
- Love the frame.

Carol Kassera
Aledo, Texas

As an active member of an artists' guild in Illinois, Carol was exposed to many different art forms, including rug hooking. She first tried rug hooking in 1970 and has hooked continually since then. Over the years she has tried and liked many different styles of rugs, but admits that her favorite is fine shading of pictorials and animals. Carol is a McGown and ATHA member. *Chocolate Chip* is her second rug to be chosen for Celebration.

Chocolate Chip, 42" x 35", #3- to 8-cut wool on monk's cloth.
Designed and hooked by Carol Kassera, Aledo, Texas, 2011. PHOTO DESIGN PHOTOGRAPHY

ORIGINAL DESIGNS

Crow

Kaye Miller is an avid bird watcher. With this design she was able to express her love of birding through her love of rug hooking. "I have done a lot of research on crows and I am fascinated by them," she says. "A lot of people think of them as sinister because of their size and color. I think of them as black beauties."

Kaye also writes poetry and penned the poem that appears on the rug. "This was a great way to show the crow with some of its good qualities," she says

With the exception of the background, the rug was color planned by Kaye.

In her original color plan, Kaye planned for a gray cloudy sky. But when she showed the rug to Jyl Clark, Jyl advised her to add silver gray green because the straight gray would dull the rug. "I have learned to take her advice as she is usually correct," Kaye says. So Kaye dyed new and recycled wool to match this new vision, using spot, dip, and casserole dyes.

The most challenging part of hooking the rug was getting the lettering just right so it became part of the rug's design and didn't fade into the background or end up too prominent. "I had to hook some of it over, and change the color of some of the pumpkins and remove the ribs [to make it all work together]," she says. "It was my first use of extensive lettering, and I enjoyed the challenge."

Kaye notes that those lessons learned through including lettering in this design are very important. "I like my rugs to tell a story," she says. She plans to use another poem in a rug for her father, an 88-year-old veteran of Pearl Harbor.

In the Judges' Words

- Great lettering.
- Loved the iridescence in the crow.
- Subtle, interesting background.
- I especially like that it's a crow and pumpkins, but it is not a cliché!

KAYE D. MILLER
LOUISVILLE, KENTUCKY

Kaye saw her first hooked rug at the Kentucky State Fair. The rug was under glass and she couldn't tell what it was made of or how it was hooked, but she knew she had to make one. Two weeks later she signed up to take a class at Cat House Rugs, a new shop opening in New Albany, Indiana. That was 2004, and since then Kaye has hooked 31 rugs, pillows, runners, stockings, coasters, etc. This rug is her second to be chosen for Celebration.

Crow, 29" x 39½", #3-, 6-, and 8-cut wool on linen. Designed and hooked by
Kaye D. Miller, Louisville, Kentucky, 2011. DONALD MILLER

ORIGINAL DESIGNS

Delightful Friends

Cec Caswell loves to put her own unique stamp on her hooked rugs. Whether it's interpreting a commercial pattern in her own colorful and unexpected way or designing a nontraditional piece, Cec looks for the brighter side of rug hooking. When she decided to create a friendship rug, it, of course, ended up being something just a little different than the norm.

"I decided to interpret it literally and design a pattern that would reflect the unique style of my hooking group. They inspire me creatively, and they provide an environment where we hook, laugh, cry, and receive support." Cec asked each of the women in the group to hook themselves and add their signature. Her job was then to hook everything in between.

So she could capture the bright colors that she loves so much, Cec dyed most of the wool herself. She used several dye techniques, including swatch, dip dye, and casserole over mostly new wool.

Cec's challenge in creating this rug was to make sure the elements remained connected. She started out with a very basic drawing on linen. She added a window. When it looked too empty, she added birds. Then she added flowers in one spot and thought they should appear in multiple areas of the rug. Colored lights became part of the border. The furniture is based on the pieces in her home. "It was important to me to maintain balance throughout," she says. "I did not want it to be so busy that it would give me a headache."

As with most of her rugs, Cec added a beaded line to frame the piece then hooked the border. She finished the edges with black yarn.

In the Judges' Words

- Fabulous! It could easily be chaotic but it's not.
- Each figure has a distinctive personality.
- Birds, baubles, and beading add to the fun of the whole piece.
- A visual delight.

CEC CASWELL
SHERWOOD PARK, ALBERTA, CANADA

Cec learned the art of rug hooking from her mother-in-law. Both her mother-in-law and her mother instilled in her a passion for bright colors. She completed her first hooked piece in 1988 and has hooked at least 50 rugs and many more smaller projects. Cec is a McGown certified teacher and belongs to the Edmonton Rug Hooking Guild. Her rugs have received a number of awards, and this rug is her fourth rug to be included in Celebration.

Delightful Friends, 46½" x 64½", #3-, 4-, and 5-cut wool on linen. Designed and hooked by Cec Caswell, Sherwood Park, Alberta, Canada, 2011. JERRY CASWELL

ORIGINAL DESIGNS

Fantasy Flight

This rug holds deep personal meaning for Lyle Drier. Shortly after being diagnosed with a blood cancer five years ago, she started attending weekly meditation where the facilitator used visualization to take the participants into a meditative state. One day, he encouraged them to ride a hot air balloon high above the Earth. An idea for a rug started to form in Lyle's mind, and she finalized it later at a workshop with Pris Buttler.

The colors in the rug were inspired by real life. While the rug has a fantasy feel in the idea that hot air balloons could fly so high, the ties to reality are emphasized by the colors Lyle chose for the Earth and the balloons. She picked the border color after the rug was completed. "I wanted something dark and rich that would complement the interior but not distract."

All of the colors for the balloons were dip dyed by Pris. The Earth's water is a combination of dip-dyed and solid color wools, also dyed by Pris. Lyle hooked the land masses with wool from her stash and stewed a recycled black wool for the sky.

The most difficult part of this composition was keeping in mind where the light was coming from and shading not only the balloons, but also the Earth, accordingly. Because those elements are spherical, the light has to touch one area brightly then fade away as the edges curve away and recede into the background.

To increase the feeling of depth that is often associated with space, Lyle allowed the edges of some of the balloons to break into the border. The technique heightens the illusion of depth that Lyle introduced in the shading of the balloons and the Earth.

In the Judges' Words

- Fabulous use of color! The balloons and the Earth look realistic.
- Contour and depth is shown in all the motifs giving everything the feel of motion.
- This artist has spent time researching this project.
- Demonstrates great control of light source.

LYLE DRIER
WAUKESHA, WISCONSIN

Lyle started hooking rugs after she saw an article in Woman's Day magazine and thought, "Wow. Those would look great in our home with our antiques. I think I'll try making one." Lyle made several, then took a 15-year break to explore weaving and other handwork. She started again in 1989 and has hooked a total of 145 projects. Lyle has received many awards for her rugs, including seven appearances in Celebration.

Fantasy Flight, 40" x 29", #3- to 6-cut wool on monk's cloth.
Designed and hooked by Lyle Drier, Waukesha, Wisconsin, 2010.

ORIGINAL DESIGNS

Geronimo

Grace Collette designed this rug as a tribute to the loved ones in her life. "My dad used to sing to my mother (the bluebirds of happiness in the tree) as she played the piano. Their favorite song was 'There's a tree in the meadow with a stream drifting by / I carved upon that tree I'll love you 'til I die.' I added my grandson to complete the picture of people I love."

To color plan the rug, Grace started with the blue water of the stream and the green leaves of the tree. She then added the complementary orange bathing suit. The yellow sky adds a feeling of warmth on a sunny day. Her final step was to work as many complementary colors as she could into the bark of the tree. "I chose to do them in a pearlescent manner, using the complements of the colors in the rest of the rug (yellow, green, and blue)," she says. "So I used purple, red, and orange of the same values, which made the whole rug come together and sing."

Grace dyed wool for all of the elements she calls the "feature items," such as the willow leaves, the bathing suit, and the bluebirds. She then filled in around them from her stash of wool.

To add dimension to the piece, Grace tried several new techniques. She added small and large glass beads to create sparkle in the water, novelty yarns for the clouds, and needlepoint yarn to emboss between the leaves. Proddy flowers add greater depth and dimension to the foreground of the piece.

Her finished piece hangs over the bed in the guestroom—until her grandson is old enough to have a home of his own.

Geronimo, 22" x 30", #3-cut wool on linen.
Designed and hooked by Grace E. Collette, Raymond, New Hampshire, 2011. ANNE-MARIE LITTENBERG

In the Judges' Words

- A memory piece well done.
- Great directional hooking and movement
- The artist has captured the motion of the Geronimo jump.
- Colors are super, especially in the blending in the tree trunks and the hanging willow foliage.

Grace Collette
Raymond, New Hampshire

Grace counts herself fortunate to have received lessons from Ruth Hall about 40 years ago at the local YWCA, but then she had to take a 35-year hiatus from hooking when life intervened and left no time for the pleasures of hooking. Now retired, she is able to work on her rugs regularly and has completed six to date. She has won a number of blue ribbons, and this is her second rug to be included in Celebration.

ORIGINAL DESIGNS

Hellebores

Kerri Kolbe loves flowers. "I enjoy gardening and find that flowers not only have an extraordinary array of colors but also forms," she says. "I love how beautiful they are both close up and from afar. I'm amazed how they change over the course of their life."

With so many flowers to choose from, Kerri drew her inspiration from a *Better Homes and Gardens* magazine spread on the earliest blooming flowers. A gorgeous photograph of hellebores by photographer Bob Cardillo caught her eye.

Kerri discovered several other reference sources and color planned the rug based on a realistic interpretation. Judy Fresk spot dyed the wool to match.

Kerri faced several challenges in completing this rug. The first was structural. Because the rug is actually four separate parts that form a whole, she had to figure out how to flow each component from one panel to another so that all four panels worked together as one piece of art. Another challenge came from trying to duplicate petal movement and the contours so that each petal gave the impression of a live, real flower. Finally, she wanted to make sure that the background did not overwhelm the hellebores but stood on its own as an integral part of the panels.

Kerri overcame all of the challenges she faced and finished each of the four panels by attaching them to wooden panels. They hang together in the living room of a summer house. Her favorite part of the completed rug is, of course, the flowers. "I love how you can feel the folds of each petal and how the center is textural and three-dimensional," she says. "The colors are vibrant and it gives both a contemporary feel while having a traditional form."

In the Judges' Words

- Nice use of color and embellishment.
- Unique method of mounting a hooked piece.
- Subtle, silvery lavender-mauve color family is different and lovely.
- Very well executed.

KERRI KOLBE
BOLTON, CONNECTICUT

Kerri started rug hooking classes with Judy Fresk just last year after seeing an article about Judy in the local newspaper. In that one year she has hooked four rugs. Recently retired from a career in information management at a large financial institution, Kerri finds that she enjoys creating images and forms using color and textures. Hellebores *is the second rug she hooked, and Celebration XXII is the first contest she has entered.*

Hellebores, 16" x 24" wall hanging in 4 panels, #3-cut wool on linen.
Designed and hooked by Kerri Kolbe, Bolton, Connecticut, 2011.

ORIGINAL DESIGNS

Kristen in the Adirondacks

For Anne Bond, rug hooking is often more about capturing memories than anything else. In designing this rug, Anne's goal was to memorialize in wool a specific element of her daughter's college career at Plattsburgh State University.

"I designed this rug as a folk art pictorial for my daughter Kristen," she says. "She spent four years in the Adirondacks playing collegiate hockey. This was her graduation present and it is packed with family memories."

Steve DiFranza drew the design for Anne, who transferred it to a linen backing. She dyed wool to create the custom colors for the ice and snow and blended in some dip-dyed wool. "By creating different tones in the wool I was able to get the effect I was looking for," she says. The result was a mottled surface that showed a variation in the colors of the ice and snow as they reflected the wintry sky above. The metal of the skates are pieces from a charm bracelet.

Anne is hard-pressed to choose a favorite part of this rug. The figures on the ice represent her children—David, the goalie, and Tressa, the figure skater—and one of Kristen's college friends. The family's three dogs, Polaris, Lucy, and Putter, sit in the foreground. The horse is Jazzy, which the family had when Kristen was born. The church is from Middlebury, Vermont, where Kristen's hockey team visited. The tree is from Rockefeller Center in New York City. But by hooking memories throughout the entire rug she sees the whole scene in its entirety—and everything it represents—when she looks at it.

Anne finished the rug with cording, and the completed piece is currently displayed in her daughter's bedroom.

In the Judges' Words

- Successful at evoking the atmosphere of a winter afternoon.
- Nice use of color and textures.
- Figures and horse well executed.
- Displays the artist's talent to create the pond, the movement of the skaters, distance, and snow.

Anne Bond
Northville, Michigan

Anne Bond started hooking rugs in 2001 when a friend showed her a finished rug that she had created. In the 11 years since, Anne has hooked 71 rugs. A cosmetologist and owner of Visions Spa Salon, Anne finds that she enjoys the diversity and creative challenge of hooking rugs of all styles. She has published dye formulas in Ewenique Dye Books I and II. Kristen in the Adirondacks is her second rug to appear in Celebration.

Kristen in the Adirondacks, 41" x 31", #3-, 4-, and 5-cut wool on linen.
Pattern drawn by DiFranza Designs; designed and hooked by Anne Bond, Northville, Michigan, 2011.

ORIGINAL DESIGNS

Mr. "GQ"

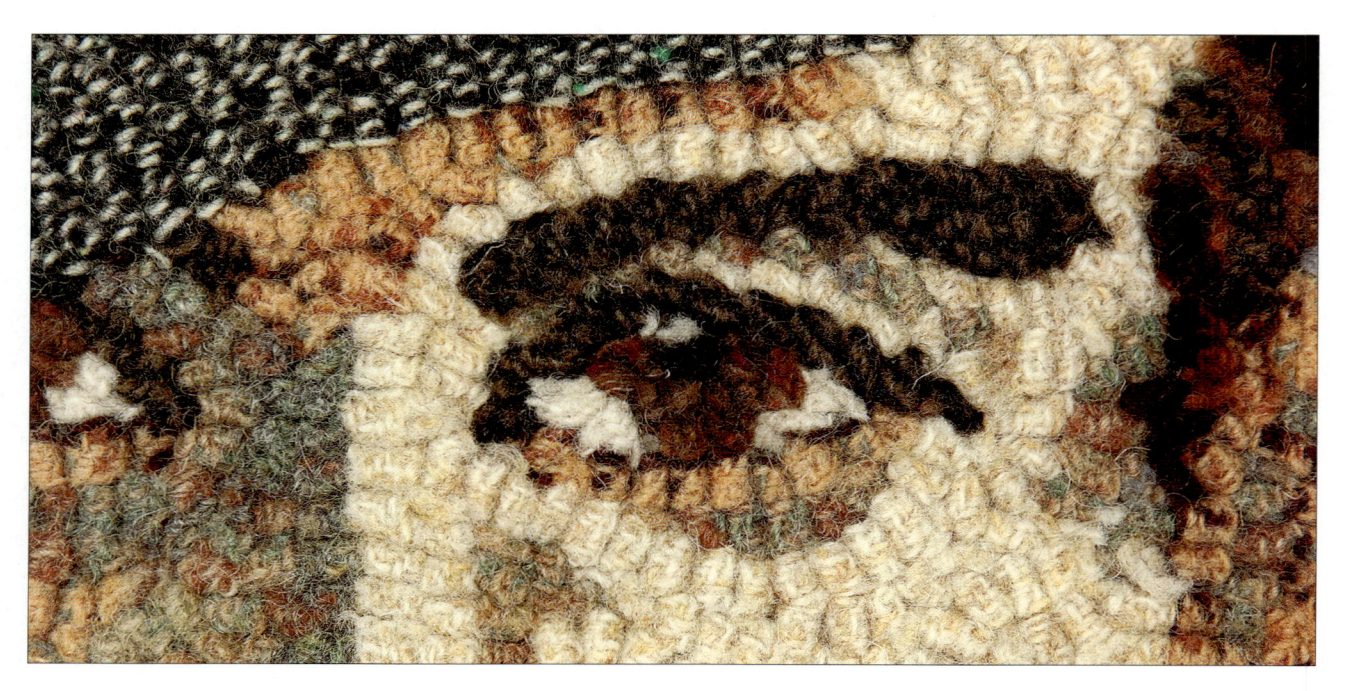

Judith Rippstein designed this rug as a personal challenge. She wanted to see if she could create a realistic portrait of a human face using wide-cut strips and off-the-bolt textured wools—not value swatches.

To choose a face for her project, Judith watched television commercials and looked at advertisements in magazines. She sketched a young man's face and named the rug Mr. "GQ" thinking that his face could be one of those featured on the pages of the stylish men's magazine, Gentlemen's Quarterly.

Judith color planned the rug based on the textured wool she had on hand in her stash. For the sky, she over dyed an oatmeal texture in two values of blue.

Creating the shadows in the face and under the chin using only off-the-bolt textures was a steep challenge. "In order to achieve the lines and shadows needed," she says, "I separated my textured wool into three stacks: one of light value wool, one of medium wool, and the last of the darkest values. Then I used from the different stacks accordingly." The different values created by the hooked loops of the textured wool allowed her to balance the highlighted and shadowed areas of the face.

Judith's favorite part of the rug is the gentleman's eyes. The warm brown color translates into a penetrating and serious, but not unwelcome, stare.

Judith finished the rug with yarn, whipping the edges with different colors to match the different background areas. The rug hangs in her hallway and will travel with her as she teaches a class on hooking faces in wide cuts.

In the Judges' Words

- Well done.
- Wonderful use of textures to create the design in a wide cut.
- A fine, distinctive portrait.
- Very successful use of textures; confident, creative, sure.

JUDITH RIPPSTEIN
FREDERICKSBURG, TEXAS

Judith grew up in Saudi Arabia where her home had all cement floors that her father covered with beautiful Persian rugs that he collected. Some, she remembers, dated back to the 1850s. When she moved to Texas in 1999, she discovered that she could learn the art of rug hooking and create her own. Judith is a McGown certified teacher and a member of ATHA and McGown. Her work has been chosen for Celebration four times.

Mr. "GQ," 12″ x 15″, #6- and 8-cut wool on linen.
Designed and hooked by Judith Rippstein, Fredericksburg, Texas, 2011. MARC BENNETT/WHITE OAK STUDIOS

ORIGINAL DESIGNS

My Happy Captain in Metz

Sunny Runnells finds that hooking something personal makes a finished mat more meaningful to her. Portraits and landscapes that she knows and loves are her favorites, and she was able to combine both in *My Happy Captain in Metz*.

"I found a wonderful photo of my husband and then chose another photo that would bring back great memories for both of us," she says. "When we retired, we bought a canal boat in Europe and now spend our summers on the boat. The background is the view we had from our back deck when we moored in Metz, France."

To combine the two photographs, Sunny altered the direction of the light in the background of the landscape photo so it matched the direction of the light shining on her husband's face. Otherwise, the difference in the two photographs would have been glaringly apparent, resulting in a mismatched design.

Sunny started the face at a portraits class with Laura Pierce. "I like that my idea of combining two photos worked, but I guess I'm most pleased that the portrait looks exactly like my husband," she says. "His eyes squint when he's really smiling, and his teeth are not shiny white."

One of the most difficult areas of the rug to hook was the reflection of the clouds in the water. "I couldn't tell how stylized they should be," she says. "Laura suggested the few simple white lines."

Sunny allowed Mother Nature to color plan her rug, and she used spot dyes, dip-dyed swatches, and as-is wool. Most of the wool is new, with some recycled wool used in the trees. The completed rug hangs on a wall shared by their dining room and family room.

In the Judges' Words

- I like the spontaneous feel of the portrait. I feel like I know the guy.
- Good depth and detail in background behind the main figure.
- The frame around this picture suits the piece with all the bits of color.
- Great emotion achieved in facial expression, especially for a wide cut.

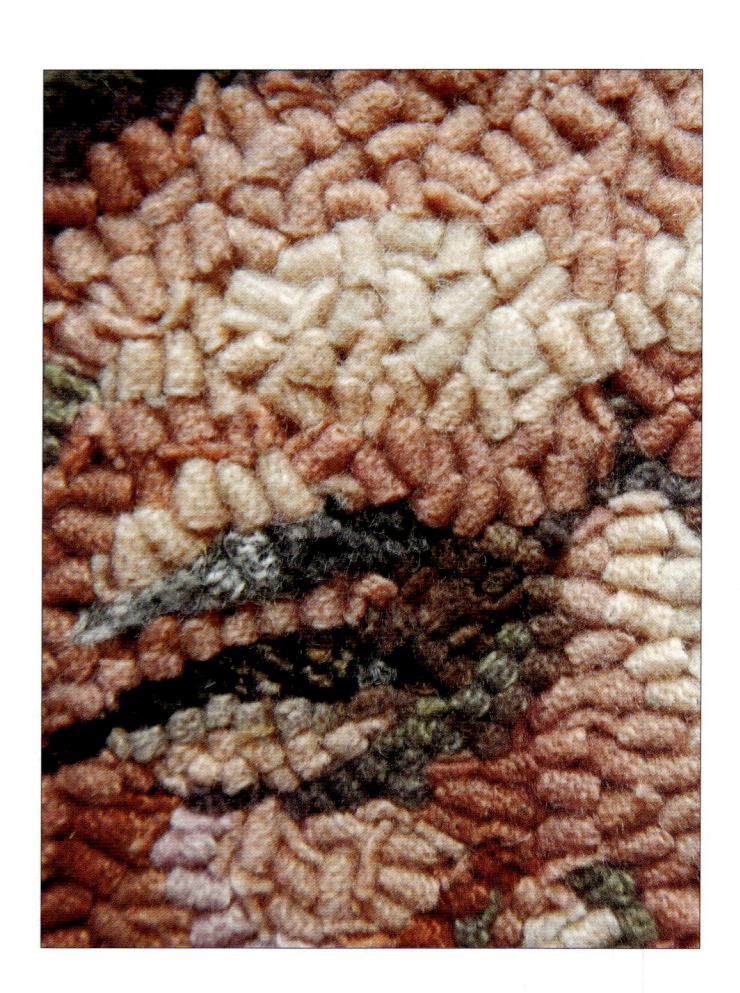

SUNNY RUNNELLS
LANTZVILLE, BRITISH COLUMBIA, CANADA

A rainy day and a good friend with a basket of worms was all it took to get Sunny interested in rug hooking about 10 years ago. A retired school teacher, Sunny enjoys hooking as well as dyeing. She is a member of the Dogwood Traditional Rug Hookers and regularly attends rug camps and classes. The inclusion of My Happy Captain in Metz *marks her first rug hooking award.*

My Happy Captain in Metz, 16 1/2" x 21 1/2", #6-cut wool on linen.
Designed and hooked by Sunny Runnells, Lantzville, British Columbia, Canada, 2011.

ORIGINAL DESIGNS

Noah's Ark Sampler

Ever since she was a child, Susan Quicksall has been fascinated by the Bible story of Noah's ark and the flood. "The description of the ark, the waters, the animals, and especially the rainbow almost becomes visual," she says. "I wanted to depict my vision of the story in the compartment-like style of a sampler in this design."

To color plan the rug, Susan portrayed the darkness of the world in the bottom section. The top sections show the world as a brighter place after the floodwaters have receded and the promise is made. The borders include verses from Scripture.

Susan hand dyed the majority of the wool in this rug, using mostly solids or values and soft, muted spot dyes and dip dyes. The border golds include eight different gold combination spot dyes. The colors for the large animals were dyed as value swatches.

Susan's favorite part of the rug is also the spot to which a viewer's eyes are first drawn: the center panel. "This is the focal point," she says. "Each part of the story is somehow part of this section—the animals, water, sky, land, rainbow, and this part of the Bible verse."

The most challenging aspect of this rug was preserving a folk-art style while she hooked the animals and the water. "I did not want it realistic, fine-cut shaded," she says, "but strived for a bit of whimsy in the water and the expressions on some animals like the tiger and the monkeys."

Most of the rug is done in a wide cut, but the lettering required a narrow cut. In order to ensure that the words would be readable, she hooked in "curly rows" behind the lettering so there were no straight lines of hooked background around the words.

In the Judges' Words

- A wonderfully conceived version of the subject.
- The waves and sky behind the ark are stormy and menacing but lovely.
- The finishing technique is beautiful.
- The lettering, the animals, and the attention to little details make this piece very artistic.

Susan Quicksall
Oglesby, Texas

Susan is a self-taught rug hooker. Both of her grandmothers hooked rugs—"it was quite the thing to do in southern Louisiana"—and one of her prized possessions is one of their rugs. She tries to hook two or three rugs a year and has been hooking since 1994. Susan is a McGown certified teacher and teaches classes at rug camps around the country and at her local community college. Her work has appeared in three of the earlier editions of Celebration.

Noah's Ark Sampler, 44″ x 53″, #4- to 7-cut hand-dyed wool on linen.
Designed and hooked by Susan Quicksall, Oglesby, Texas, 2011. JOE GRIFFIN PHOTOGRAPHY

ORIGINAL DESIGNS

Patrick and Logan at Balsam Lake: Summer of 2009

Trish Johnson captured this moment in a photograph and then decided to recapture it in wool. "I was impressed with the pink quality of the light and wanted to see if I could capture it in a rug," she says.

The other aspect of the photograph she was hoping to capture was the emotion of the moment. Her son, Patrick, and their dog, Logan, had been playing with a soccer ball when the ball ended up in the lake. Patrick lifted the dog into the canoe and paddled out to fetch the ball. "I like that Patrick's attention is on the task at hand—getting the ball—but Logan has eyes only for Patrick," she says. "It is a rug about the devotion a dog has for his master."

Trish didn't plan colors for this rug. She started with the wool she had in her stash and worked forward from there. As she hooked, she found that she had all the wool she needed on hand. "I'll dye something when I need to and I like to change things as I go," she says. She used new and recycled wool plus some gray and white Lopi (Icelandic) yarn in the rug around Logan's neck.

The most challenging part of this rug was hooking her son's face. "The face is so small and the wool is so wide," she says. "You have to decide what you can leave out. You have to just hook the minimum necessary to recognize it as a face." Trish focused on using smaller cuts—#3 and #4—to give an impression of her son's face rather than a realistic interpretation.

Trish finished the rug with a ball of variegated wool that she found in her stash, letting the colors fall wherever they fell as she whipped the edges. "It reminds me of Rugby shirt stripes—sort of boyish and sporty—so it suited my purposes."

Patrick and Logan at Balsam Lake: Summer 2009, 30" x 12 1/4", #3- to 5-cut wool on linen. Designed and hooked by Trish Johnson, Toronto, Ontario, Canada, 2010.

In the Judges' Words

- Well done pictorial that captures both boy and dog.
- Finishing is interesting and suits the piece.
- Great show of color to indicate motion in the water.
- Admirable shading on the boat.

Trish Johnson
Toronto, Ontario, Canada

It was 1973 and Trish was 21 years old when she learned to hook rugs from her aunt. Her aunt was hooking a rug featuring the famous schooner, the Bluenose, and Trish ended up hooking a lot of the sky for her. She picked up a hook again in 1990 and has completed 40 rugs since then. She is interested in sky, the weather, lights and shadows and likes to hook in an Impressionistic style. She is a teacher and a member of four guilds. This rug is her sixth to be chosen for Celebration.

ORIGINAL DESIGNS

Pennsylvania

Jan Winter has been interested in Pennsylvania Dutch arts and Fraktur paintings for many years. A class with Fraktur expert and rug hooker Susan Feller provided the inspiration for this rug.

Jan's first thought was to use only Pennsylvania barn hex signs, but she decided on a pattern of circles similar to one she had seen on a piece of furniture. She placed a kaleidoscope in the center, added circles and stars from the era then encased it all in a naturalistic border of heart and vines.

Jan planned all the colors but went through many changes, especially where the background was concerned. At first she dyed parchment-colored wool, then she tried a lightly mottled wool for a watercolor look. Both efforts seemed too pale. She overdyed a houndstooth and cream wool texture with a slightly darker tone, but decided it was still too light to support the darker reds and oranges. She finally found an off-the-bolt stripe that had the perfect texture and depth of color.

The simple leaves of the vine border were a challenge. "Even though I had stacks of what appeared to be different values of green wool, after hooking them in, they all looked the same," she says. "Then I added blue to the leaves, but it stood out too much or faded to nothing. My final choices had more brown than blue in them."

When all was said and done, Jan's rug took about four months to hook. She finished it with a whipped border through monk's cloth and twill tape. "I've found it's best to have lots of textures and value changes to add interest," she says.

In the Judges' Words
- Lovely soft design.
- Great use of color.
- Wonderful geometric details.
- Interesting center background texture.

Jan Winter
Hollywood, California

Jan started rug hooking in 1992 after she took a quilting class called Hooked on Appliqué. *A fellow student shared the book* American Hooked and Sewn Rugs, *and "when I saw the pictures I just had to make the real thing." Jan has completed 23 rugs to date, mostly in a primitive style. She has received several blue ribbons for her work.* Pennsylvania *is her eighth rug to be chosen for* Celebration.

Pennsylvania, 32" x 48", #6- and 8-cut wool on monk's cloth.
Designed and hooked by Jan Winter, Hollywood, California, 2011.

ORIGINAL DESIGNS

Remembering Spring

Cheryl Bollenbach often designs rugs around thoughts that weigh heavily on her mind. *Remembering Spring* is a story rug that came to her after a visit to a nursing home.

To bring the story to life, Cheryl placed an elderly woman at the center of the design. A much younger version of her husband, as evidenced by their matching gold bands, stands behind her. Cheryl's use of shades of gray opens the door for the viewer to draw his or her own conclusions about this gentleman. Has he passed away? Is he ill?

Cheryl did all of the color planning and dyed all the wool for this project. She used some as-is wool, but most of the wool was dyed specifically for this project or pulled from her studio shelves. She incorporated metallic embroidery floss to outline the paisleys on the woman's scarf and roving to make the woman's hat three-dimensional.

Cheryl began hooking this rug in March 2011 and by mid-April had hooked just the woman's face and hat. She hung the rug on a wall in her studio while she worked on other projects. By July she was ready to start again and finished it in four months. "This is the first time I have ever let a rug hang in a place where I could look at it every day and in all types of light," she says. "It let me firm up some ideas about what I wanted to do with the rug."

The quilt had originally started out as a blue blanket, but Cheryl realized she needed a space to reflect the colors from the background and the main figure. She also shortened the verbiage around the edge and reworked the border. "I never mind ripping out to get the effect I really want," she says.

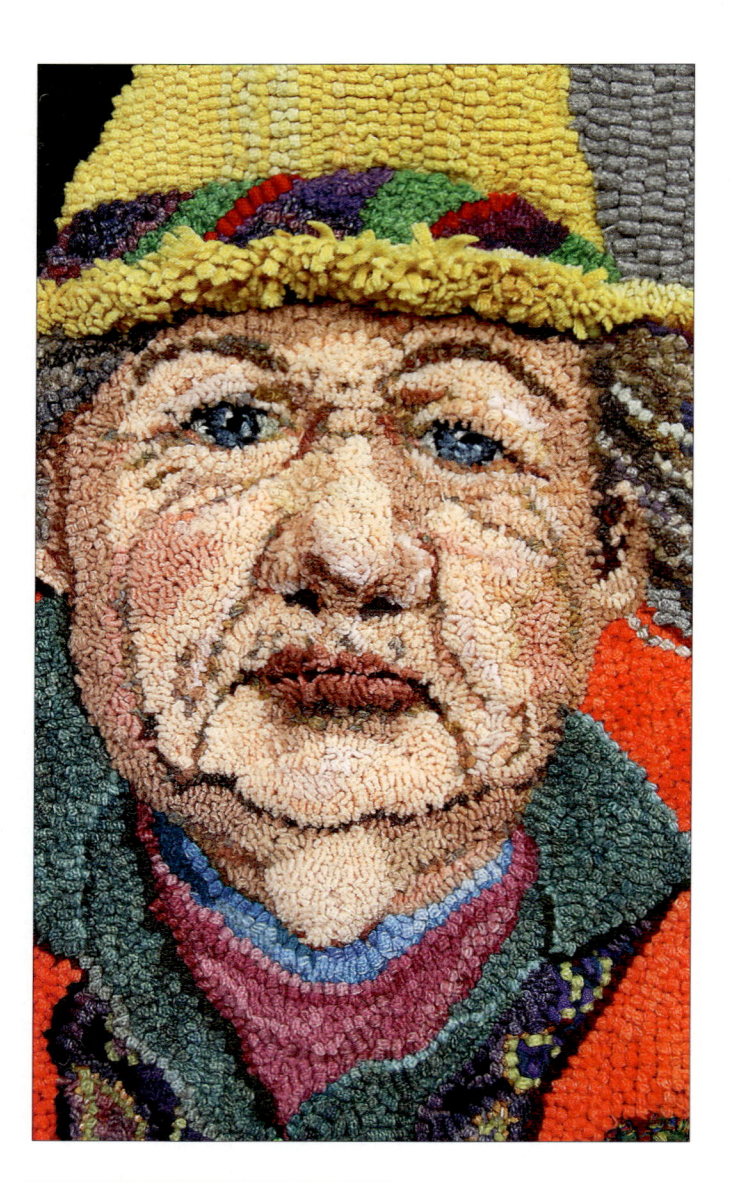

In the Judges' Words

- *Without a doubt one of the best pieces I have ever seen—from the techniques used in sculpting to the emotion the piece elicits from the viewer.*
- *Fabulous details and use of color.*
- *Those hands are wonderful, and I just love all those wrinkles.*
- *The sentiment is thought provoking.*

Cheryl Bollenbach
Golden, Colorado

Cheryl watched local rug hooker Patty Martinson demonstrate rug hooking every year for three years before she convinced herself to pick up a hook in March 2005. Her first experience was with a crochet hook, a pair of scissors, a scrap of uncut wool, and a piece of burlap. Now she is willing to try all sorts of techniques and has hooked 33 mats, rugs, and pillows. Cheryl is a member of the National Guild of Pearl K. McGown Hookrafters and the Colorado Rug and Fiber Guild. This rug marks her first appearance in Celebration.

Remembering Spring, 31" x 50", #3- to 8-cut wool on linen. Designed and hooked by
Cheryl D. Bollenbach, Golden, Colorado, 2011.

ORIGINAL DESIGNS

Sorrow

Ivi Nelson Collier is intrigued by the two sides of the human face. When she envisioned this rug, she saw gold feathers and a face that did little more than anchor the corner of the design. "I wanted a design that would give me both parameters and freedom to explore color and this unusual way of looking at the face," she says. "I chose the unusual dimensions for added interest and challenge."

Ivi carried the idea of the rug around with her for a long time before she felt ready to commit it to paper. She color planned the rug with the help of Sandra Brown, who encouraged her to create "zones" throughout the rug. She used dip dyes and casserole dyes over new and vintage wool to create the colors she needed. The wool was cut into various widths. "There are also several non-wool fibers used sparingly throughout for a little sparkle," she says.

Ivi's favorite part of hooking her own design is the process itself. "I do research and pull lots of loops and lots of wool to see how they look," she says. In this rug, she loves the movement of the colors and the luminous effects they generate.

Her biggest challenge in creating this rug did not come until after the rug was hooked and finished. "The constant diagonal nature of the hooking created problems that were not apparent until the rug was hanging," she says. "While it is hooked and finished on the straight of the grain, the linen stretched and one side is longer than the other. I've steamed and steamed again, nailed it to a frame to dry, and re-whipped the bottom. I finally accepted that this is the nature of this piece."

In the Judges' Words

- *Beautiful control of color and shape in the wings.*
- *Face exhibits the name of the design.*
- *Wonderful movement and blending of colors in the hair.*

IVI NELSON COLLIER
NOTTINGHAM, MARYLAND

Ivi learned about the Internet and rug hooking at the same time—in 2004. Now she finds it hard to imagine how she ever got by without either of them. She estimates that she has created dozens of rugs in the past eight years. She is a member of ATHA and hooks with several groups. Sorrow *marks her first showing in* Celebration.

Sorrow, 18" x 36", #3-, 4-, and 6-cut wool on linen.
Designed and hooked by Ivi Nelson Collier, Nottingham, Maryland, 2011. ANNE-MARIE LITTENBERG

ORIGINAL DESIGNS

Still Life #8— The Bowl of Onions

Carol Koerner relies heavily on photography as a tool for planning her rug hooking pieces. When she's working on a still life, such as *The Bowl of Onions*, she takes several photographs of the real-life set up, then she compares the shots and chooses the best angle, lighting, and composition. When she hooks portraits, she takes photos without a flash to get high contrasts and well-defined features.

In putting together the still life subject for this rug, Carol had three things in mind. First, she chose onions because of "their really cool skins and tails." Second, she wanted to hook the antique salt-glazed bowl that had belonged to her husband's grandmother. And finally, "I thought it would be fun to hook that red stripe in the old tea towel."

Carol found the color planning for this piece easy because she wanted to duplicate the colors exactly as she photographed them. "The only color decision left to me was whether to have a dark or light background," she says. "I chose dark because the dark brown and gray would make the subject matter stand out."

Her favorite part of the finished rug is the onion in the foreground. "I just enjoy looking at this onion with the tail and the split in the skin showing the yellow onion beneath," she says.

"As with all my still lifes, I set myself a challenge to depict a new and different texture," she says. "Here it was the luminescent skin of the onions. Meeting the challenge hooking them directionally, feathering in the different shades. The highlights give the skins a realistic shine."

In the Judges' Words

- Great composition in a still life—effective shadowing.
- Beautiful painterly piece of rug hooking.
- Attention to detail: contrasts, highlights, and shadows.
- Loved the essence of the still life and the reality of color in a simple, everyday object.

Carol Koerner
Bethesda, Maryland

Carol's parents began hooking about 15 years before she decided to try rug hooking. "I never dreamed that after years of watercolor and pastel painting I would be hooked, but here I am, in love with creating art by pulling little woolen loops through linen backing." Carol has finished 36 pieces in the past 16 years. She is a member of ATHA and has won numerous ribbons for her work. The Bowl of Onions marks her eighth appearance in Celebration.

Still Life #8—The Bowl of Onions, 16$\frac{1}{2}$" x 21", #3-cut wool on linen.
Designed and hooked by Carol Koerner, Bethesda, Maryland, 2011.

ORIGINAL DESIGNS

Summer Winds

Mix together a good friend, a pair of floral linen pants, and a rug hooker who loves challenge. The result is *Summer Winds*.

"I had the pants lying on a table in my workspace," says Bea Brock, "when a friend saw the side seam where a flower went in one direction on one side of the seam and in another direction on the other side. She said she liked that kind of movement, and if I designed it, she would buy it."

So Bea designed the pattern. Her friend did not buy it, but Bea loved the movement enough to want to hook the design herself. She color planned the rug based on the colors she had available in her stash, then dyed a background wool to complete the rug.

Her favorite parts during the hooking were the two floating leaves in the opposite corners. "They were great fun to pull colors for and create a watercolor-like blending," she says. "Very satisfying to hook."

The most challenging aspect of the project was preserving the movement of the design. Without the movement, Bea feared the result would be staid and the resulting rug would be less attractive. She worked to keep everything going by using a multitude of tones in each area.

Bea worked steadily on the rug and completed the hooking in about six to eight weeks. Unfortunately, the binding took just as long. She rolled the edge around cording and used a hand-dyed rug yarn to match the final row of loops. The piece remains rolled up until Bea can paint the upstairs hallway to match the color scheme of the rug.

In the Judges' Words
- Lovely design.
- Great fluidity and movement in the flowers.
- Calm and peaceful.
- Love the design of the rug—lots of movement, very whimsical.

Bea Brock
Kerrville, Texas

Knowing that her youngest child would head off to kindergarten in Fall 1995, Bea began to look around for an activity to fill her newfound alone time. She saw a hooked rug in the window of a quilting store and started taking classes immediately. In the past 17 years, she has hooked around 40 rugs. Bea is a McGown certified teacher and a member of ATHA. This rug is her second to be featured in Celebration.

Summer Winds, 35" x 45", #8-cut wool on linen. Designed and hooked by Bea Brock, Kerrville, Texas, 2011.

ORIGINAL DESIGNS

Swamp Critters

Swamp Critters,
14" x 84", #6- to 8-cut wool and embellishments on linen. Designed and hooked by Corinne Watts, Washington, DC, 2010.

SHARON TURNER PHOTOGRAPHY

Corinne Watts knew she was up for a challenge when she responded to a call for entries for a gallery show at the Bluebonnet Swamp Nature Center in Baton Rouge, Louisiana. The show, A Walk Through the Swamp, included artwork by the Contemporary Fiber Artists of Louisiana, and each of the pieces entered in the show was to be hung from the ceiling and visible from all sides as visitors walked among them. Corinne's answer to the challenge was to create a long, skinny rug—just over 1 foot wide and 7 feet long.

Coming up with a design to fit those measurements proved to be another challenge. Corinne started from the ground up, showing an alligator, an armadillo, three turtles, a heron, a raccoon, and an owl. "It's hard to select any one animal as my favorite," she says. "Each one revealed its own personality as they all came alive on the rug, and it was great fun to see how each developed."

Because the piece would be viewed from all sides in the gallery, Corinne had to finish the entire back as well. She chose a camouflage wool from Gail Dufresne and focused on piecing the fabric so one tree trunk ran the full length of the piece. To finish the edges, she brought the fabric to the front and stitched it in place next to the hooking to create a narrow border. The completed rug hangs from wide camo tabs that slide over a piece of swamp branch.

A closer look at the piece shows some of the extra touches that Corinne added to the rug: labradite stones; glass, wood, and shell beads; silk organza and mohair yarn; and wool cutouts.

In the Judges' Words

- *Interesting embellishments and techniques.*
- *A fun piece.*
- *A fine rug that succeeds on all levels.*
- *The colors are just right and the use of textures is inspired.*

CORINNE WATTS
WASHINGTON, DC

Corinne grew up in a family that loved to do many types of handwork. She occasionally came across a hooked wool rug in the South, but it wasn't until she moved to Washington, DC, that she realized there were instructors and classes available. Her first class was at the Smithsonian Institute in 1999 and she has hooked 25 rugs of varying sizes since then. She is a member of ATHA, and Swamp Critters *is her second rug to appear in* Celebration.

ORIGINAL DESIGNS

The Grand Canyon

Designing a specific rug for a specific spot in a specific house is not always easy. Often it takes waiting for a stroke of inspiration, which is what hit Mary Jo Lahners when she was looking for an idea for a rug for her daughter-in-law's room. It was her bedspread, of all things, that sparked Mary Jo's creativity

"Kathy wanted a long rug to go above her bedroom dresser," Mary Jo says. "After looking at the colors in her bedspread, I thought of the colors in the Southwest and then thought, 'The Grand Canyon would cover all the colors.'"

Mary Jo studied a handful of pictures online to work out a color plan for the rug, but none seemed like they would work well with her rug. "I didn't have a clear idea of how it would look, so I just looked at the picture in my head," she says.

After much consideration, she decided to color plan the rug using all striped, plaids, and checks to make the different levels of the ridges. "I liked using them because someone else had done the work for me in deciding if the colors will work together," she says. "By careful cutting, I could make the mountain ridges come alive." To make the cliffs stand out and separate the foreground from the background, Mary Jo hooked them in vertical lines.

Because Mary Jo wanted the hooking to continue to the very edges of the rug, she opted for no border and instead bound the edges with the wool in the rug. The completed rug now hangs in its prescribed spot in Kathy's bedroom.

In the Judges' Words
- Beautifully executed.
- Clever, and a great use of textures.
- Love the way the lettering is included in the sky.

Mary Jo Lahners
Lincoln, Nebraska

Mary Jo has hooked more than 60 rugs in the past 13 years. She enjoys rug hooking because it is a forgiving art, but she says the real joy "lies in meeting some of the most wonderful people in the world and having a gift our loved ones can enjoy through the years." Mary Jo is a member of ATHA and has won numerous ribbons for her work. The Grand Canyon marks her first appearance in Celebration.

The Grand Canyon, 29 1/2" x 21", #7- to 8 1/2-cut wool. Designed and hooked by Mary Jo Lahners, Lincoln, Nebraska, 2010. DAVID DALE

ORIGINAL DESIGNS

Toolbox

Anne-Marie Littenberg finds inspiration in the world around her. "I am falling in love with the elegance of the everyday," she says. "I find beauty in mundane elements, like the elements of a box of tools."

She designed this rug after watching her husband, Ben, preparing to take on another task around their home. Her perspective is unique, focusing on the tools and the hands that will use them rather than on the entire person and the project he plans to undertake. The viewer is left to ponder what this man might be making and why.

Anne-Marie included many materials other than wool in this piece. She incorporated plied threads of wool, silk, cotton, polyester, lurex, rayons, and more which went through a cotton backing. The mix of materials allowed her to get the shading and the texture that she needed to depict the scene realistically.

While the background and the shirt hooked up smoothly, Anne-Marie found her greatest challenge in hooking the contents of the toolbox. "Keeping the tools distinct in the toolbox required a lot of concentration," she says. "I decided to focus on one tool at a time and not worry about the whole thing because it seemed too overwhelming to do so. Once I got one screwdriver done, it was time to move to another tool."

The finished rug was very heavy, something that Anne-Marie didn't anticipate when she started the project. To ensure that the piece wouldn't be compromised if hung just from a sleeve, she lined the back of the rug with cotton muslin using a technique similar to that which museums use to help stabilize and maintain the weight of ancient tapestries. It is currently on display in her dining room.

In the Judges' Words

- *Draws me in and makes me want to meet this man.*
- *Loved the detail and depth in the toolbox.*
- *Arresting point of view.*
- *Blending from pale gold to lavender in the background is wonderfully subtle.*

Toolbox, 36" x 36", plied threads of silk, wool, cotton, polyester, etc. on woven cotton. Designed and hooked by Anne-Marie Littenberg, Burlington, Vermont, 2011.

ANNE-MARIE LITTENBERG
BURLINGTON, VERMONT

Anne-Marie admits to "always fiddling with fiber." She has been hooking rugs for 20 years but has only been at it seriously for the past 12 thanks to a move to Vermont and an involvement in the Green Mountain Rug Hooking Guild. With her days of administrative jobs and 60-hour workweeks behind her, she now focuses on hooking, photography, and writing. Anne-Marie is a Celebration winner and the recipient of the Sauder Village Award.

ORIGINAL DESIGNS

Wedding Dance

Eric Sandberg spent almost 30 years in Hollywood as a motion picture costume supervisor. His rug, *Wedding Dance*, is inspired by the period films on which he worked. The details are pulled from his personal costume library, books, and paintings.

"The colors are right, but although I tried to capture the bold patterns, my skill was not enough," he says. "I only have a little of my costume library left," he says, "but I still have several reference books on European Renaissance and Restoration theater costumes. Parts of the design were inspired by the work of 16th century artist Jacques Callot."

Eric color planned the rug himself. The dancing figures were hooked with leftover swatches and dip dyes from other projects. The rest of the wool came from what he calls his "snarl bag," a collection of garbage containers, plastic bags, cardboard boxes, and baskets that hold all leftover strips from the wool he dyes for his students. "If I hooked diligently every day for the rest of my life I couldn't use up what I have," he says.

Eric had a deadline to work by, and after a year of thinking about how to render the piece, he didn't leave himself enough time to hook the piece properly. "I did a lot of reverse hooking, and it slowed me down more," he said. "I literally mapped the piece out on butcher paper and blocked off how much I had hooked that day."

The completed rug is finished with rope cording and tassels. It will travel with him to teaching engagements across the country. His biggest lesson learned? "That I always do my best work under pressure."

In the Judges' Words

- Interesting and unusual choice of subject.
- Figures are great, especially the one with the beak (upper left) and the one in rose-colored tights.
- Shows motion, perspective, color knowledge; a painterly piece of art.

Eric Sandberg
Athens, Georgia

An avid needleworker, Eric picked up a hook at a flea market in Los Angeles in 1992 and taught himself to hook. In the years since, his to-do list of fiber art projects has adjusted to contain only rug hooking projects. He is drawn to older designs and larger projects, and his goal is to finish one rug a year, even if it's just a small teaching piece. His work has been displayed nationally and in Japan. This rug is his second to be chosen for Celebration.

Wedding Dance, 28" x 38", assorted-size wool strips on linen.
Designed and hooked by Eric H. Sandberg, Athen, Georgia, 2011.

ORIGINAL DESIGNS

With Closed Eyes

With a little bit of trepidation and a lot of adventure, Judy Cole jumped right into the process of designing *With Closed Eyes*. Her goal was to set free her inner artist and design a rug on pure inspiration. Her friends just thought she was crazy.

"My eyes are closed and my heart is pounding," she says. "The marker is in my left hand—by the way, I'm right-handed. I am about to draw my largest rug to date directly onto my backing."

When she opened her eyes to take a look at what she had drawn, Judy hesitated. "What I saw was sweeping curved lines intersecting across the fabric in unrecognizable ways," she continues. "What have I done? Where do I start?"

That's when she sees the first recognizable shape in the pattern: an egg. "It's true," she says. "Given enough time to observe, this mind begins to see hidden objects."

Judy's experiment in creativity continued as she bypassed the color planning stage and just started hooking bits and pieces of the rug as shapes revealed themselves to her. She hooked the egg first in red and green. Then she discovered a bird, then a woman's head and torso, then a fish and a turtle.

Judy allowed the rug to grow from there and finished it within four months. "Working on inspiration can be exhausting," she says. "I allowed the rug to grow, not knowing what would appear next. I had a ball. It was my favorite rug to hook.

"I identified with the woman," she says. "She was me, free without boundary, moving into new and wonderful art worlds. But no one thinks I'm crazy anymore—just adventurous."

In the Judges' Words
- Well done technically.
- Loved the beading.
- Certainly original. The artist knows what's happening here; the rest of us will just have to enjoy a treat for the eyes.

With Closed Eyes, 62" x 63", #8-cut hand-dyed and as-is wool on linen. Designed and hooked by Judy Cole, Shelburne, Vermont, 2011. ANNE-MARIE LITTENBERG

JUDY COLE
SHELBURNE, VERMONT

Judy learned to hook three years ago at the local high school. With 30 rugs hooked, Judy has found a path to express her creativity—one that she is still exploring. Judy belongs to the Green Mountain Rug Hooking Guild and ATHA. She attends workshops and hooks weekly with friends. She has won numerous ribbons for her work. This rug marks her first appearance in Celebration.

HALCYON YARN

HALCYONYARN.COM 800•341•0282 – CALL FOR YOUR FREE CATALOG
Drop by our shop in Bath, Maine or follow us on Facebook & Twitter!

100% WOOL * SPUN & DYED IN THE U.S.A.

Halcyon Signature Rug Wools
Available in three styles: Classic, Deco & Geo. Dozens of colors ~ perfect for every project!

Everything you need for hooking, punching & edge whipping.
Discover the full line of rug wools plus tools, books, projects and inspiration!

SHOWCASE OF
Commercial Designs

A rug hooked from or substantially based on an existing commercially produced pattern.

COMMERCIAL DESIGNS

8-Cut Rose

Ellen Jensen enjoys working with the very largest strips, anywhere from a #8-cut to a #10-cut wool. This pattern by Jane Olson allowed her to test her shading skills while using wide cuts.

Ellen admits to spending quite a bit of time looking at swatches dyed by Nancy Blood before choosing one for the rose. "We decided on Hot Pink—bright enough to keep me excited and calm enough that Nancy didn't go blind dyeing the wool," she says. "I remember Nancy saying that some days she needed to wear sunglasses in her kitchen."

In the Judges' Words

- *Well-executed shading skill. Looks so real.*
- *Good example of how to shade a rose with many values in an 8-cut!*
- *Dramatic as all get-out. I love being surprised, and these colors with this execution and this daring choice of background do it.*

Nancy dyed all new wool, including one textured wool from England. The swatches for the leaves used the same three dyes as the background and were dyed over a Dorr green, a Dorr bright turquoise, and a Dorr British green tweed.

Those leaves turned out to be the most challenging part of completing the rug. Ellen drew them on paper and worked out the shading with colored pencils before she hooked them into the backing. "This method saved me a lot of pulling out wool," she says, "which I really dislike doing."

The center of the rose was also a difficult area to envision and then hook. She wanted her use of the swatches to convey the depth at the center of the rose so that overall the entire rose would appear three-dimensional.

Ellen needed 15 skeins of tapestry wool to bind the rug. She chose to combine three colors from DMC—Ultra Dark Bright Khaki, Ultra Very Dark Brown, and Ultra Very Dark Pecan. The finished rug hangs in her sunroom where she does most of her rug hooking.

8-Cut Rose, 36" x 36", #8- and 9-cut wool on monk's cloth.
Pattern by Jane Olson; hooked by Ellen M. Jensen, Martinsburg, Pennsylvania, 2011. LEIDY STUDIO

ELLEN M. JENSEN
MARTINSBURG, PENNSYLVANIA

Ellen said no to rug hooking for many months until one day she decided to see firsthand what it was about this new craft that had her dear friend so excited. "Needless to say, I was hooked as soon as I entered the classroom." Ellen has completed more than 90 pieces since 1978. She currently uses wider cuts almost exclusively and prefers a "folk art" look rather than a true primitive. Her work appeared in Celebration XVIII as an honorable mention.

COMMERCIAL DESIGNS

American Kestrel

Sheila Mitchell was invited to teach this design by Jane McGown Flynn at the Western McGown Teachers 2010 Workshop in Eugene, Oregon. "I had hooked birds before and really enjoyed the challenge to create realism with rug hooking," she says.

Sheila tweaked the pattern just a bit to tell the story of this American kestrel hunting on the edge of a farm field in late summer. The bird has chosen an ideal perch on a weathered fencepost and is poised to watch the entire field spread before him.

The color plan for this rug was definitely a function of the bird and its setting. "I color planned using two complements to create this piece: dark orange and blue-gray as well as yellow-green and red-violet," she says. "The color plan had much to do with the gender of the bird (adult male) and the season (late summer/harvest)."

Sheila chose value dyeing over new wool for the kestrel and spot dyeing for the field and the leaves in the foreground. She painted the wool for the mountains using a very weak solution of the same blue formula used for the kestrel mixed with a mordant. She darkened some strips by applying a weak formula of the dark orange to create a gray-brown tone. The mountain colors echo the colors of the kestrel. A few strips of recycled and textured wool give the fencepost and rail a rugged look.

"I think I successfully captured the alert and intense look in the kestrel's eye, so I have to say the favorite part for me is the head and all its detail." The most difficult parts were rendering the wing and tail feathers. Sheila had to eliminate much of the detail while retaining a hint of individual feathers.

In the Judges' Words

- Subtle but effective composition and coloring.
- The kestrel is well done, especially in the wing area.
- The bird is very lively, and the colors soft and pretty.
- The hooker has skillfully managed to allow the bird's head to stand out against mountains and sky.

Sheila Mitchell
Victoria, British Columbia, Canada

Sheila became interested in rug hooking after a trip to Nova Scotia but couldn't find much information about the craft when she returned home to Victoria. So she taught herself and has been "unlearning" a lot of bad habits ever since. She began devoting time to rug hooking 14 years ago and has hooked more than 40 pieces. She is a member of Woolly Thyme Rug Hooking Group. This rug is her second to be featured in Celebration.

American Kestrel, 16" x 20", #3-, 4-, and 5-cut wool on cotton rug warp.
Pattern by Jane McGown Flynn; hooked by Sheila Mitchell, Victoria, British Columbia, 2010. JOHN MITCHELL

COMMERCIAL DESIGNS

Anatolian

Jeanne Benjamin will teach just about any pattern, but when it comes to hooking for herself, she chooses Orientals, antique-looking primitives, or pictorials. She had printed a pattern of *Anatolian* for a customer but decided to hook it herself when she discovered that the pattern was not quite square on the fabric.

Jeanne prefers to hook Orientals using a traditional Oriental palette. "Since my last two Orientals had a red or blue field, I went with golds for a change," she says. "The three golds are three different formulas of mine that worked out well when I mixed them together and hooked them in small areas. One is gold, one is bronzy, and the third is a dull orange."

When she started hooking this rug, Jeanne didn't have a detailed color plan drawn up. "I started in the middle (after choosing the background) and just chose from my pile of wool as I went," she says. "Contrast is essential; more so for the main motifs. I trust my eye and use it. If my first choice doesn't have that certain charisma with the rest of the wools, I change it." The result was a rug that almost hooked itself.

Jeanne likes the design of this rug overall, but her favorite parts are the two different border designs on the short ends of the rug. The left edge features a repeating geometric pattern while the right edge incorporates flowers and V-shaped accents. "I saved them for the end," she says. "That was a creative way to finish the rug."

Anatolian, 48" x 27", #4-cut hand-dyed wool on linen. Pattern by New Earth Designs; hooked by Jeanne Benjamin, Brookfield, Massachusetts, 2011. JEREMIAH BENJAMIN

In the Judges' Words

- I like the gold background with the degree of variation and the way it (and the red) is repeated throughout the multiple borders.
- Beautiful fringe.
- Good detail and movement in the color fields.

JEANNE BENJAMIN
BROOKFIELD, MASSACHUSETTS

Jeanne and her parents all started hooking rugs in 1971. Her mother worked at Lincoln House in Sturbridge, Massachusetts, where the McGown business was located at the time, so Jeanne purchased the basic equipment and took lessons there. Jeanne estimates that she has hooked at least 150 rugs and more than 100 small pieces. Since 1989, she has traveled the country to teach at camps and workshops. Anatolian marks her fifth appearance in Celebration.

COMMERCIAL DESIGNS

Cape Shore Crewel

Fran Oken's quest to learn the art and technique of fine shading in one of Nancy Blood's classes led her to this pattern by Joan Moshimer. Nancy directed her class to choose flowers, fruit, or crewel, and Fran picked crewel. "The grace and fancifulness of this pattern attracted me immediately," she says.

To color plan the rug, Fran sent Nancy a sample of the colors she wanted to use and Nancy placed them on the rug for her. Nancy invented a spot dye named after the rug and used it to dye 8-value swatches for everything except the background.

Of the many elements that make up this rug, Fran enjoyed hooking the squirrel, butterfly, and owl the most. "They bring balance to the rug," she says. "They are living creatures existing quite naturally in a fantasy world of gnarled miniature trees, unusual flowers, and giant multicolored leaves."

Hooking the large leaves with internal shading proved to be the most challenging part of the rug. "There were many values of one color in the center. The problem was how to blend them in a natural way," she says. "I kept rehooking the leaf until it had the desired effect."

To finish the rug, Fran corded and whipped the edges with a wool yarn that matched the swirls in the border. The completed rug hangs above the fireplace in her living room. "I learned much about shading, tapestry, hooking, and finally, perseverance," she says. "The constant in my life was *Cape Shore Crewel*."

In the Judges' Words

- *Nice interpretation of a crewel design.*
- *Like the subtle loop detail around the edge.*
- *This is a killer rug. I love drama in a rug, and it's here.*
- *The detail and shading are perfect.*

Fran Oken
Rutland, Vermont

Fran managed to avoid the rug hooking bug for one and a half years under the guise of not wanting to involve herself in another craft, but she finally succumbed and took lessons from Jean Evans. She has hooked 18 pieces in the past 14 years, including stools, portraits, and floor rugs. Fran is a member of the Green Mountain Rug Hooking Guild, the Northeast Kingdom Rug Hookers, and McGown Rughookrafters. Her acceptance into Celebration *is her first rug hooking award.*

Cape Shore Crewel, 55" x 39", #3-cut hand-dyed wool on rug warp.
Pattern by Joan Moshimer; hooked by Fran Oken, Rutland, Vermont, 2010. ANNE-MARIE LITTENBERG

COMMERCIAL DESIGNS

Daghestan Prayer Rug

Cathy Williams watched over a fellow rug camper's shoulders as this pattern by Jeanne Benjamin came to life. "After watching the student's progress for five days, I loved the pattern more and more."

Cathy asked Nancy Blood to color plan the rug for her. Nancy used just seven colors that were spot dyed in abrash. The reds, golds, and blues reflect the vibrant, saturated colors for which Nancy is well known.

Cathy's favorite part of the rug was hooking the 45 shields in the center of the rug. The motifs are randomly arranged by color, and in each motif, all seven colors are used. Cathy's challenge was to keep the colors balanced while not repeating them. No two motifs are exactly the same.

Another challenge with this rug came with the inner and outer borders and the flowers shown there. Even though she used #3-cut wool, she still struggled to squeeze in all the detail. Cathy outlined each flower and then outlined the four inner petals. She randomly filled the petals with one color and chose a second color for the flower's center. With the exception of the diagonal line at the corners, all the stitches in the border are hooked in a straight line

The fringe that finished the rug is made from the rug's rug warp backing. She first sewed six rows of herringbone stitch next to the last rows of stitching. She removed the wool threads from the top and bottom border edges below the herringbone rows and took groups of four warp threads at a time to tie off as a fringe.

Cathy hopes the rug will eventually belong to her eldest grandson.

In the Judges' Words

- Beautiful. An enormous accomplishment.
- Excellent use of color and repetition throughout the rug.
- Great execution of the woven effect in an oriental.
- Very vibrant colors used and balanced within the piece.

Cathy Williams
Los Gatos, California

A teacher has been instrumental in giving Cathy a solid foundation in rug hooking. She has completed 50 pieces in 20 years. While she hooks many styles of patterns, she prefers fine, tapestry hooking. Cathy is a McGown member and a member of the Tin Pedlars and the Peninsula Rug Hooking Guild. Daghestan Prayer Rug marks her first inclusion in Celebration.

Daghestan Prayer Rug, 41" x 66", #3-cut wool on rug warp, fringed with rug warp.
Pattern by Jeanne Benjamin/New Earth Designs; hooked by Cathy Williams, Los Gatos, California, 2011. EVAN TCHELEPI

COMMERCIAL DESIGNS

Eden's Floor

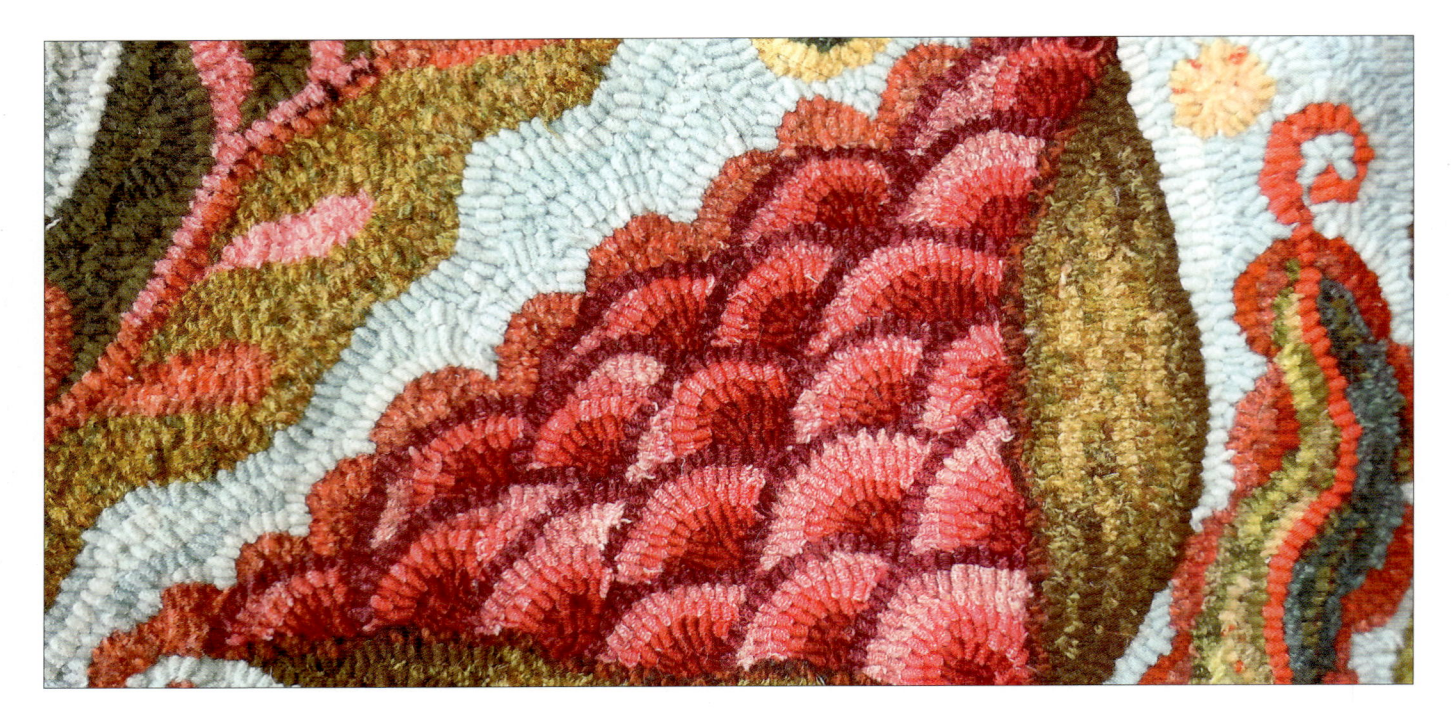

Carol Lynn Gillingham loves color play. "I don't believe I have ever chosen to hook a rug for a particular place in my home," she says. "Rather I choose it to use a new textured wool I have found, or maybe because there are two values that would look great hooked together."

And that's how it went with *Eden's Floor*. Carol saw a beautiful color scheme in a needle-punched piece and asked rug hooking instructor Bea Brock to plot those colors into a pattern for *Eden's Floor*. She was captivated by the decorative flowers and the whimsical leaves, as well as the opportunity to work color after color into the rug.

"Bea knew I wanted the background to be the blue color," she says. "Her challenge to me was to take the color plan she gave me and choose the wool that would make her color plan come to life."

One technique Carol learned to meet that challenge was to use three shades of a color instead of just one in any chosen area of the rug. The gold in the leaves is a perfect example.

When the rug was finished, she decided that those large leaves were her favorite parts of the rug. "I departed from the color plan when I hooked these leaves and struggled with color choices," she says. "It was very satisfying when they were complete and added so much to the overall look of the rug."

Carol finished the rug with a herringbone stitch. She didn't think about where to display the rug until after it was finished, and she is currently working on identifying the perfect spot.

In the Judges' Words

- Interesting color choice; it really works.
- Wonderful play and repetition of color.
- Border treatment sets off the rug very nicely.
- This rug has a playful quality that is most appealing.

Carol Lynn Gillingham
Helotes, Texas

Carol picked up her first rug hooking project after seeing the art being demonstrated at the Folklife Festival in San Antonio, Texas, and has hooked 24 rugs in the past 18 years. Her first teacher was Angela Pumphrey. Carol is most comfortable hooking with a #6 cut but has used everything from a #3 cut to a #8 cut. This is her first rug hooking award.

Eden's Floor, 30" x 51", #6-cut wool on linen.
Pattern by Bea Brock; hooked by Carol Gillingham, Helotes, Texas, 2011.

COMMERCIAL DESIGNS

For Your Love

For Connie Bradley, rug hooking is a time-honored tradition that she shared with her mother. Connie remembers watching her mother hook rugs when she was around 10 years old. It makes sense then that Connie finds herself drawn to the older designs in general and some of Jane McGown Flynn's classics in particular. "I dabble in creating my own patterns but love many of the older McGown patterns because of their detail," she says.

Connie found the detail in the flowers in this rug striking. She lists roses, lilies, daisies, and bluebells among her favorite flowers, and the realistically colored center motif caught her attention. The scrolls around the border are also a type that she has hooked before.

Connie color planned the rug herself. She chose to double swatch the flowers—a technique her mother taught her—to get good depth of color in the petals. For the background she used a mixture of many greens overdyed for movement. With the inclusion of lighter greens, the background seems to dance behind the flowers. All of the wool for the scrolls was dip dyed to be just a bit paler so the flowers would be the focal point of the rug.

Connie clipped the corners of the rug to give it a different shape. She bound the rug with a herringbone stitch. She often puts a piece of macramé cord inside the burlap and stitches over it before applying the binding tape in an effort to keep the loops at the edge from being crushed.

In the Judges' Words

- Good shading techniques applied.
- Beautifully executed dip-dyed scrolls.
- Wonderful highlights on the edges of the rose petals!
- A very nicely done interpretation of a very traditional rug.

Connie Bradley
Wellington, Ohio

Connie hooks rugs for relaxation, a creative outlet, and enjoyment. She and her mother became McGown teachers about 12 years ago. She enjoys teaching a variety of styles. Connie belongs to the Lorraine County Hookcrafters. Her rug's selection for Celebration is her first rug hooking award.

For Your Love, 29" x 51 1/2", #3- and 4-cut wool on burlap.
Pattern by Charco Patterns; hooked by Connie Bradley, Wellington, Ohio, 2011. DANIEL MESSAROS

COMMERCIAL DESIGNS

Grenfell Goose

Leslie Cuthbertson chose this traditional Grenfell pattern as part of a class project with Joan Foster at the Prairie Harvest Rug School. Her love of color led her to change the background from traditional browns to a glowing sunset. Instead of a stylized Grenfell goose, she opted to keep the same shape but hook the bird in silhouette.

Leslie color planned the rug with Canadian sunsets in mind. In keeping with Grenfell tradition, she used pantyhose to hook the rug. With the exception of the goose, Joan dyed all of the colors in the microwave in a glass pie plate covered with plastic wrap. Leslie also used bleached dark pantyhose for parts of the sky.

Leslie found the nylon pantyhose difficult to work with, which provided an ongoing challenge. "It is very thin and you have to be careful it doesn't turn on you," she says. "You also have to hook in every row and every hole. I just took my time and checked to make sure all the loops were as perfect as I could get them."

Her favorite part of the rug is the silhouetted goose against the contrast of the bright colors of the setting sun. "It reminds me of geese flying home from feeding and an Alberta or Saskatchewan sky at sunset," she says.

Leslie finished the rug in the traditional Grenfell way by turning the linen to the back, folding it under about half an inch, then blind stitching it. The whole process of creating this rug, from color planning to finishing, gave her a good look at the history of Grenfell rugs and a new appreciation for working with a material other than wool.

In the Judges' Words

- *Wonderful interpretation of Grenfell mats using the traditional stockings.*
- *Color is vibrant.*
- *Really captures the look and feel of a Grenfell mat.*
- *The loops are well done.*

Grenfell Goose, 12", pantyhose on linen.
Pattern by Grenfell Institute; hooked by Leslie Cuthbertson, Airdrie, Alberta, Canada, 2011.

Leslie Cuthbertson
Airdrie, Alberta, Canada

For years, Leslie's mother encouraged her daughter to learn how to hook rugs, but with two children in sports and a full-time job, Leslie couldn't find the time to devote to the art. When she met a woman demonstrating rugs at a local exhibition—someone who also knew her mom—Leslie decided it was time to start rug hooking. She finds the artform rewarding and has completed 10 rugs since 2004. Grenfell Goose is her first award-winning rug.

COMMERCIAL DESIGNS

Jumbo Star

Janet Griffith first saw a rug hooked from Lib Callaway's *Jumbo Star* pattern at a Yellow Rose Rug Camp several years ago. When she returned to the camp she worked with Gene Shepherd to color plan her own version of the rug.

"I changed a few of the motifs on the outside border for more of a 'cabbage rose' look," she says. "Gene suggested the dark red center and also to proceed with lighter reds to gold/orange at the tips."

Janet took a large variety of wool from her own stash to camp. She purchased a dark red for the center, a dip-dyed piece for the background around the quilt motif, and a bit of green. Janet mottled most of the wool. To create the red to gold/orange tips, she used a dye method in which she poured the colors at opposite ends to make a third color in the middle.

Janet used the strongly contrasting light and dark backgrounds to give the rug a dramatic effect. She found hooking the striped border to be the most challenging aspect of the rug because of the quick alternations between numerous colors. Making sure the circle stayed a circle was also a challenge.

Janet finished the rug with bias-cut wool strips from one of the brown background colors and placed the completed rug in her kitchen nook. She has no trouble identifying her favorite part. "I love how the rug sunbursts out from the center with the vibrant colors," she says. "It makes me happy."

Jumbo Star, 34" x 34", #7-cut wool and paisley on linen.
Pattern by Lib Callaway; hooked by Janet Griffith, Frisco, Texas, 2011.

In the Judges' Words

- *Great balance in color plan—moves my eyes around.*
- *Beautiful looping.*
- *Lovely color plan and easy to live with.*
- *The colors are harmonious and balanced.*

JANET GRIFFITH
FRISCO, TEXAS

Janet attended a rug hooking class in 1992 when the promise "NOT latch hook" caught her eye. She stopped counting how many rugs she'd hooked when she hit 200 in 2005. Janet is a McGown certified teacher and a member of ATHA. Jumbo Star's inclusion in Celebration marks her first rug hooking award.

COMMERCIAL DESIGNS

Leaf Border Geometric

Find Linda Gustafson something large and floral, and she's right there with her hook. "I am drawn to large rugs and I am drawn to floral rugs," she says. "I really liked the border on this rug. That's what caught my eye first when I saw this design."

Linda planned the colors for this rug based simply on her personal preferences. "My favorite colors are red/orange, turquoise and lime/green," she says. "I love the way they look together, and I use them a lot in my rug hooking. That's really the main reason I chose these colors for this rug—I like them!" Linda also likes to work with bold textures. She employs lots of honeycombs, houndstooth, and herringbone wools in her rug projects.

Collecting all the wool for the rug took Linda quite a bit of time. She does not enjoy dyeing but rather searches for new and recycled wool for her projects. All of the wool for *Leaf Border Geometric* was purchased whenever and wherever she found just the right texture and color. "When I see a piece of wool that really speaks to me, I usually buy it then because I'll probably never see anything just like that again," she says.

Throughout the border of this rug, Linda was able to apply her favorite hooking method: use of textured wools. When in doubt, she finds textured wools are a fail-proof go-to. They served her well in the leaves because she was able to mix a number of textures.

The most challenging part of this rug was hooking the flowers. Because they are so large, Linda found herself changing colors and using lots of contrast to break up the space within each floral motif. Her lesson learned? "I found out that hooking large flowers isn't as easy as it looks," she said.

In the Judges' Words

- Vibrant colors used well.
- Great use of textures and movement in background.
- I like the jewel-like colors and the freedom of execution in this rug.
- Great color play and balance.

Linda Gustafson
Chardon, Ohio

About 19 years ago, Linda stumbled upon a rug hooking demonstration at a county fair. The rest, she says, is history. She doesn't keep count of her rugs, other than to see that she considers the year a successful one if she can complete two large rugs and a couple of small rugs. Linda belongs to several state and local guilds. Her work has been featured in Celebration twice.

Leaf Border Geometric, 32" x 51", #8½-cut wool on linen.
Pattern by Port Primitives; hooked by Linda Gustafson, Chardon, Ohio, 2010. PASTOR PHOTOGRAPHY

COMMERCIAL DESIGNS

Pemaquid Lighthouse

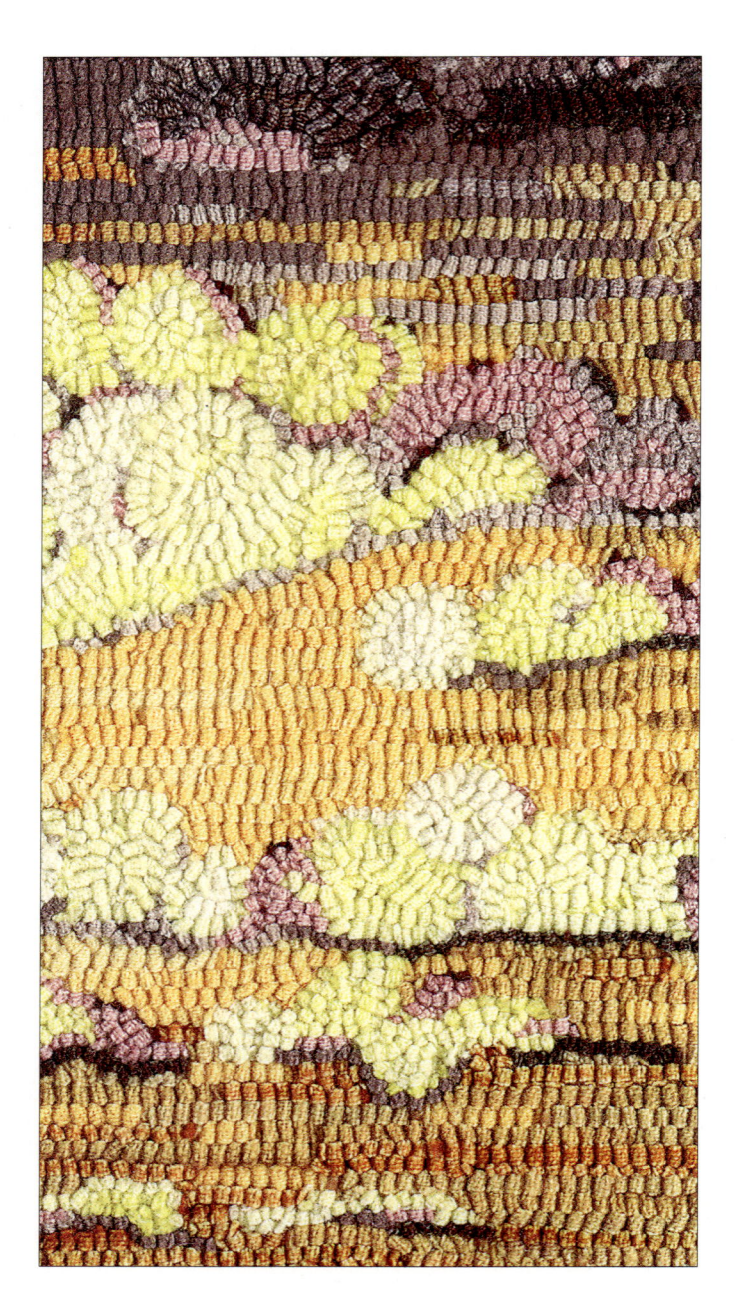

Ellen Forstrom will tell you herself that the thought of hooking some rugs just bores her to tears. "A rug I hook doesn't need to be original, but it does need to be interesting," she says, "so I am always interested in new dye techniques or new hooking techniques.

When she picked up this traditional lighthouse pattern from Jane McGown Flynn, she decided to forego the usual daytime scene with a bright white lighthouse beside a vivid blue ocean; she decided to attempt a silhouetted lighthouse at sunset. She planned the colors based on a photograph that her daughter, Katelyn Cahilly, had taken of the sun setting directly behind the lighthouse at Peggy's Cove in Nova Scotia.

Most of the wools to match the colors in the photo were easy to find. All of the blacks in the rug are as-is wool, most of the strips in the foreground were leftover from other projects, the sunset is a straight degradation dye over white, and the ocean is overdyed green and blue plaids. The sky, however, was not so easy.

"As I considered what a night sky looked like," she said, "I decided that it looked almost like this drab piece of wool but not quite. So I threw it into several dye pots to see which one would make the best sky. What I discovered was that they all make a great sky when hooked together."

The large purplish cloud at the top right ended up being the most difficult part of the rug, from her first attempt at hooking it to the final incarnation. It was either too whimsical or too bright or too distracting. Ellen finally decided to hook it to match the sky. "I can't say that I love that cloud," she says, "but it will do."

In the Judges' Words

- Captured the essence of the lighthouse with both movement and stillness.
- Visually exciting and technically well executed.
- Unusual choice of color for the sky.
- Bold interpretation of the sky, sun, and clouds.

Ellen Forstrom
North Haledon, New Jersey

Ellen discovered rug hooking about 20 years ago when she researched a lovely Cheticamp rug that her sister had found in a gift shop. What she saw was enough to send her to her first rug hooking camp. Her most ambitious project to date is a 5-foot by 6-foot flower rug that took 5 years to complete and was featured in Celebration in 2007. Ellen is a nurse on a Rapid Response Team and belongs to the Midland Park Rug Hooking Group.

Pemaquid Lighthouse, 24" x 36", #3-, 4-, and 5-cut wool on rug warp.
Pattern by Jane McGown Flynn; hooked by Ellen Forstrom, North Haledon, New Jersey, 2011. BILL BISHOP

COMMERCIAL DESIGNS

Rugs by the Sea

Jo Ann Hendrix enjoys hooking commercial designs, but she's also very fond of tossing in a few of her own adaptations to personalize the rug she's working on. *Rugs by the Sea* is no exception.

Jo Ann added several items to this pattern by Beverly Conway, including the rug draped over the porch and the miniature rug show on the lawn. And "if you look closely, there is a small piece of bright pink yarn held by a mischievous raccoon who, according to tales, lives under the porch," she says.

After color planning the rug, Jo Ann dyed wool to match her ideas. She used spot dyes and abrash along with textured off-the-bolt wool. The directional hooking in the rug helps to establish the strong lines of the inn against the sky and the lawn.

She notes that hooking the miniature rug show was the most challenging part of the rug. One of the rugs had to be just right because it was hooked by a friend and appears in an earlier edition of *Celebration*. "I accomplished the desired results by perseverance," she says.

To finish the rug, Jo Ann used cotton rug tape and whipped the edges with yarn. It occupies a display space on the wall in her den where she changes out rugs according to the season. *Rugs by the Sea*, of course, hangs there during the summer months.

Jo Ann has been hooking primarily wider cut designs over the past few years. "This rug made me realize that I still really enjoy the challenge of hooking detailed pictorials," she says.

Rugs by the Sea, 29³/₄" x 26³/₄", #3- to 5-cut wool on linen.
Pattern by Beverly Conway; hooked by Jo Ann Hendrix, Pasadena, Maryland, 2010. STEVIE TRISHMANN

In the Judges' Words

- Wonderful use of color.
- Very impressed with amount of detail shown in piece.
- Charming design. Fine use of color, attention to detail, and execution.
- Vertical and horizontal hooking is effective in delineating the architectural details.

Jo Ann Hendrix
Pasadena, Maryland

Jo Ann, a retired home economics teacher, finds that rug hooking provides a means of self-expression, hours of enjoyment, and many friendships. She started hooking rugs about 16 years ago after taking a class taught by Roslyn Logsdon. She is a member of the Anne Arundel Rug Hookers, and the Mason-Dixon Chapter of ATHA. Her rugs have been exhibited at the Maryland State Fair, the Anne Arundel Rug Hookers rug show, and the Montpelier Arts Center. This rug marks her third time in Celebration.

COMMERCIAL DESIGNS

Victorian Garden

Judy Colley loves flowing designs. This pattern, designed by Roche Riverhouse, fit the bill perfectly. Judy immediately fell in love with the serrated leaves, the large multilevel flowers, and the trumpet-shaped blossoms. "My mind started color planning before I even had the pattern fully unfolded," she says

To choose her colors, Judy started with a list of all the colors she liked. "It seemed to scream for bright colors," she says. "I started thinking of all the colors I liked that would connect well and dyed them in a dip-dye fashion so the colors flowed from one to another on the same piece of wool."

Judy knew the background for the piece had to be dark to set off the bright colors. "I dyed brown and purple in spotted pieces of wool," she says. "I hooked the background last in little clusters and then went back and connected the clusters. I learned to do backgrounds this way from Nancy Blood."

Judy used an outline-and-fill method to hook the flowers and the leaves, following the contours of the designs. Her color changes are gently shaded in some areas, but on other areas of the rug, she opted for bold color shifts.

The background was the most time-consuming area of the rug to hook. She used a random fill to help the flowers stand out even more from the field of browns behind them.

Judy hooks daily, which makes rug hooking a very big part of her everyday life. "I hook three hours every night, which is 21 hours a week," she says. "It also means I have 21 favorite television shows."

In the Judges' Words

- *Effective subtle crewel. Love the bottom leaves.*
- *Technically handled very well in the use of color, placement, excellent shading.*
- *Nice use of transitional swatches to interpret the design.*
- *Pastel colors against a dark background are very appropriate for the design.*

Judy Colley
Wyoming, Michigan

Judy has been hooking rugs for 40 years and places her number of completed pieces somewhere between dozens and hundreds. She started out hooking fine shaded rugs and figures she has done most everything else since then. Judy is an accredited McGown teacher, co-director of Off the Ocean Rug Hooking Conference and On the Lake Rug Hooking Conference, and teaches at home and on the road. She is a member of the McGown Guild and ATHA.

Victorian Garden, 36" x 47", #4-cut wool on linen.
Pattern by Roche Riverhouse Designs; hooked by Judy Colley, Wyoming, Michigan, 2011. BILL BISHOP

THE WOOLERY

Your Fiber Arts Supplier Since 1981

Helping you Hook, Spin & Weave for 30 Years!

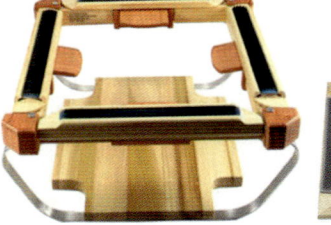

Spinning Wheels & Supplies - Felting Supplies - Rug Hooking - Knitting - Looms & Weaving Supplies - Braiding - Kumihimo

Frames - Bee-Line, Snap Dragon, Gruber, K's Creation, Searsport & more.

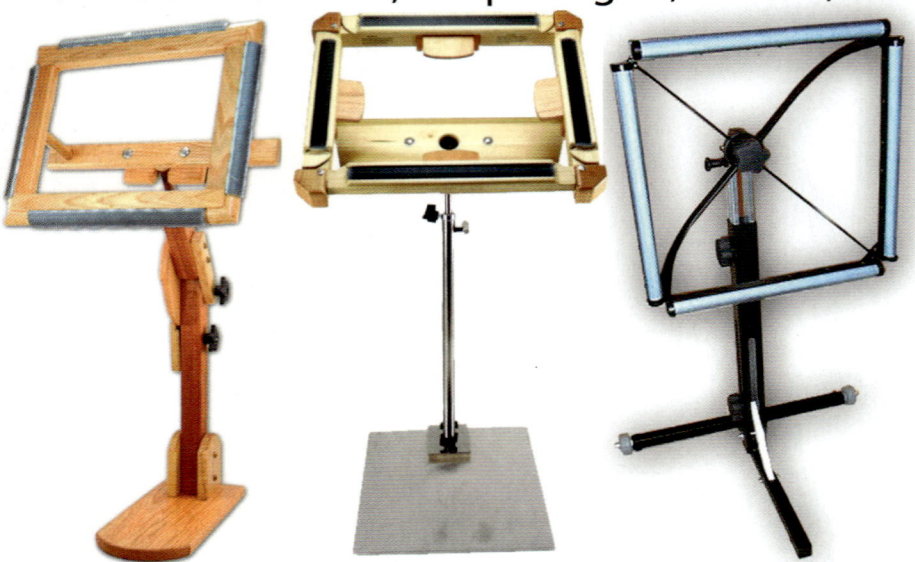

Hooks - Hartman, Nancy Miller, Fraser, Searsport & more.

Yarn

Cutters

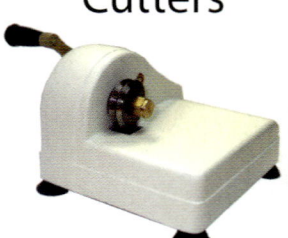

Rug Hooking Kits

Join us on Weavolution
Join us on Ravelry
Like us on Facebook
Watch us on YouTube
Get Our Newsletter
Follow us on Twitter
Read Our Blog

www.woolery.com
800-441-9665

Free Shipping!* *Orders Over $100. Some items excluded due to mfg.'s restrictions. Out of State orders save KY Sales Tax! LeClerc Looms eligible for free shipping but discounts are excluded. Call us or check our website for more details.

Save on Yarn & Fiber
Spend $100 Get 10% Off.
Spend $200 get 15% Off.
Spend $300 get 20% Off

THE WOOLERY
(502) 352-9800 - info@woolery.com
315 St. Clair, Frankfort KY 40601

SHOWCASE OF
Adaptation Designs

ADAPTATION

A rug hooked as a copy or interpretation of a piece of work originally found in another medium. A re-creation of another's painting, photograph, postcard, or art.

Celebration XXII 2012 • 85

ADAPTATION DESIGNS

Bonneville 200 MPH Club Life Member

A special occasion often deserves a special commemoration. Betty Magan chose to hook a portrait of her husband, Shaen, becoming a 200 MPH Club Life Member for his seventieth birthday.

Interestingly enough, the actual hooking wasn't the most challenging part of bringing this rug to fruition. "It was very difficult to keep this rug a secret while I was hooking it, as I was so tempted to ask for his input," she says, "especially while working on the car. I worked on it for over two months, whenever Shaen was gone."

As far as the actual hooking goes, the face and hands were the hardest areas to capture because of their small size, proportionally speaking. Betty remembers feeling discouraged until she had hooked enough of the surrounding design for it to all start to come together. "I had such a good response from family members I showed it to," she says, "and when the grandchildren recognized 'Bop' right away, I knew I had succeeded."

Betty's teacher, Laura W. Pierce, dyed all new wool for the rug in spot dyes and dyed swatch sets in yellows and blues. It was important to Betty that all the colors be true to the original photograph of her husband receiving his award.

"I definitely gained knowledge about hooking a face and hands," she says. 'I didn't like the way traditional hooking looked on this piece, so I learned to hook in what I call the random style. I really like the end result."

Betty framed the finished rug with a narrow golden brown inner border and a wider black border. It is tucked away under her bed—for now.

In the Judges' Words

- Captured the accomplishment in a subtle way.
- The blue band at the top of the white background was a good idea to break up the space.
- Like the "horizontality" and the "pebble-y" hooking.
- Colors are soft but effective.

Betty Magan
Bass Lake, California

An avid quilter and a recent knitter, Betty was introduced to rug hooking through a sample rug on display in a local quilt shop. In the past 10 years, she has tried all styles of hooking, from fine shading to primitive. Her only complaint is that there aren't enough hours in the day to hook as much as she would like to. Betty has attended the Cambria Pines Rug Camp for 10 years. This rug marks her third appearance in Celebration.

Bonneville 200 MPH Club Life Member, 35" x 20", #3- to 8-cut Dorr wool on linen.
Adapted from a family photograph and hooked by Betty Magan, Bass Lake, California, 2011. TOM MILNE/MILNE PHOTOGRAPHY

ADAPTATION DESIGNS

Dad

Cindy Irwin's rug, *Dad*, is a tribute to her father, who is pictured in the bottom right-hand corner. Both Cindy and her father attended one-room schoolhouses with Amish children. His school burned down in the 1960s, so Cindy combined two photos to create the pattern: one of his class and another of her schoolhouse.

Her finished piece has quickly become a family favorite because of all the nostalgia she was able to work into the rug. Cindy used one of her mother's skirts for her father's pants, his favorite tie for his shirt, a piece of her sister's wedding gown and a strip of satin from her own clothing for the flowers, and her brother's sweater for the shadows. The pump is modeled after the one behind her grandparents' home, and she added a goat because her father raised them as a child.

The finished piece is also a culmination of many of the rug hooking techniques she's learned over the years. She used hand-painted wool for the sky (Peggy Hannum) penny dyeing for the siding (Cyndi Gay), "puddling" for the tree (Eric Sandberg), combining as-is wool for the grass (Barb Carroll), trimming to create texture in the roof and hooking with one thread of wool to create detail in the faces (Joan Reckwerth), and cutting a #4-cut strip with a #3 to get a #2-cut strip that stays together (Judy Carter).

"If you ever get a chance to take a class from a new teacher, just do it," she says. "You will always learn something new, and you never know how you will use it in the future."

In the Judges' Words

- Captured the essence of the day—simple yet effective.
- Love the faces and outfits on each child.
- A super pictorial/group portrait/period piece.
- All the directional hooking makes an interesting surface, and the tree is rendered with subtlety.

Cindy Irwin
Pequea, Pennsylvania

In 1983, Cindy bought a kit and had a five-minute lesson on how to pull loops. She was interested enough to keep pursuing rug hooking on her own but didn't really get fully involved until she took a class with a teacher several years later. "It made all the difference," she says. Now Cindy is a McGown certified teacher and a juried member of the PA Guild of Craftsmen. She sells supplies and teaches workshops from her home. This is her fifth rug to be chosen for *Celebration*.

Dad, 36" x 48", #1- to 8-cut wool and satin on linen.
Adapted from family photographs and hooked by Cindy Irwin, Pequea, Pennsylvania, 2011. BILL BISHOP

ADAPTATION DESIGNS

Gold Hill, UK

Bernice Howell had one goal in mind when hooking this rug: Recreate the original photo as closely as possible with only what she had on hand in her stash. And she almost did it.

"As the old saying goes, you can have a hundred greens but never the right one. My big bag of cut green strips came in very handy with all the foliage in the background," she says. "But I did have to dye the bright green in the background fields."

The photograph that caught Bernice's eye was an award-winning shot by Clarence Carvell of an ancient cobblestone street in Shaftsbury, England. "I liked the composition of the picture with its descending row of old houses against the fresh greens of the English countryside," she says.

She enjoyed hooking the roofs and chimneys and seeing the varying effects afforded by the different textures of wool from her stash. She even found herself using pieces of wool that she thought she would never use.

Bernice found simplifying and organizing the background—and then selecting the right greens—to be the most challenging aspect of completing the rug. The task seemed daunting until she concentrated on one small section at a time.

Gold Hill, UK, ended up being an excellent example of why Bernice likes to hook rugs. "I get to work with a full palette of colors, feel the softness and textures of the fabric, and experience the 'Wow!' effect that they create. I can rework an element until it pleases me. Sometimes the challenge can be frustrating, but there is a great feeling of satisfaction when you reach your goal."

In the Judges' Words

- The perspective is great in that you know you are going down the hill.
- Contrast of color gives good depth and dimension. Colors glow.
- Beautifully rendered British town scene.
- Lovely sense of sunlight, especially in the wooded background.

Bernice Howell
Beltsville, Maryland

A desire to try something new and totally different led Bernice to try rug hooking when she retired from teaching English and speech. She signed up for a class with Roslyn Logsdon and has been part of Roslyn's Friday morning class for the past 27 years. Bernice prefers to use #3-cut wool and focuses on designing patterns that involve people or places that hold a significant place in her life. Her work has graced the cover of Celebration, and she has been chosen as a finalist several times.

Gold Hill, UK, 30½" x 20", #3- and 4-cut wool on monk's cloth.
Adapted from a photo by Clarence Carvell (with permission) and hooked by Bernice Howell, Beltsville, Maryland, 2011. JOHN D. HOWELL

ADAPTATION DESIGNS

Hawa

Jackie Roop based this rug on a painting by Laura Paige Archer, a nurse volunteering with Doctors and Nurses without Borders and a childhood friend of her son. Laura painted portraits of the patients who came to the camp for help with their illnesses, a pastime that encouraged those she was caring for and inspired her.

"I was amazed by her happy face in the midst of all she had to endure as a displaced African person," Jackie says about choosing this particular painting to hook. "She [Hawa] spoke to me."

Laura's original painting was done in blacks and browns. Jackie altered the colors to accentuate the joy in the woman's expression. Her head covering is a lively purple and the glasses take on a red appearance despite the blues, greens, and oranges mixed into the execution of the frames.

Hooking the teeth and the reflection in the glasses were Jackie's biggest challenges as she worked on completing this project. She started over many times as she tried to get both of those areas just right. In the end, the only solution was trial and error—pulling out and rehooking—until she achieved the look she was after.

Jackie used only 100% wool strips in creating *Hawa*. All of the wool, except the bandana and the glasses, is as-is wool. For the glasses, she used a spot dye.

The finished rug is stretched over artists' canvas and placed in a wide, red, vinyl-like frame. "I learned that anything is possible if you have the drive and desire," she says. "It makes me realize that I do have a God-given talent."

In the Judges' Words

- *Captured the personality of the black and white painting in subtle color.*
- *Color line at the edge of the piece is a nice touch.*
- *Great example of using as-is materials, especially in a portrait.*
- *Execution of facial details is wonderful.*
- *Background is an excellent choice.*

Hawa, 24" x 24", #4- and 8-cut as-is wool and torn strips. Adapted from a painting by Laura Paige Archer (with permission) and hooked by Jackie Roop, Charlottetown, Prince Edward Island, Canada, 2011. JOHN ROOP

JACKIE ROOP
CHARLOTTETOWN, PRINCE EDWARD ISLAND, CANADA

Jackie started hooking rugs in 1982 when her son started afternoon kindergarten. She used her newfound free time to take rug hooking lessons for $2 an hour. In her 30 years of rug hooking she has hooked more than 100 rugs in all styles, from portraits to primitives. She is a member of ATHA and the Green Mountain Rug Hooking Guild and has sold rugs to tourists as far away as Japan and Africa. Her inclusion in Celebration is her first rug hooking award.

ADAPTATION DESIGNS

Indian Boy— Ah-Chee-Lo

Many rug hookers claim to learn patience while hooking their rugs; Donna K. Hrkman learned it over and over as she hooked row after row in the blanket draped around this young boy's shoulders. "The endless rows needed to make the wool blanket look real could be tedious to do, but the overall effect was worth it," she said.

Fortunately, the repetitive nature of the blanket wasn't the first thing Donna saw when she decided to turn this 1905 photograph by Edward Curtis into a hooked rug.

"I was immediately captivated by his beautiful eyes," she said. "He seems so stoic for a young child, so serious and concerned."

To duplicate the monochromatic color scheme created by the sepia tones in the original historic photograph, Donna chose a plum-colored brown. She dyed her wool in eight shades of a single dye to ensure that she had enough variation to adequately capture the boy's facial features.

Working with a historic photo presented another challenge, too. Parts of the photo from which she was working were blurred or indistinct, so some of the boy's hair was difficult to reproduce. "I just followed my instincts and let it work itself out," she said

When she was done the contrast between the boy's hair and the rigid lines of the blanket turned out to be her favorite part of the rug.

"I hook because I've found that it's the perfect combination of my favorite things: color, line, and texture. I feel like I'm creating a lasting piece of art that expresses my love for beauty."

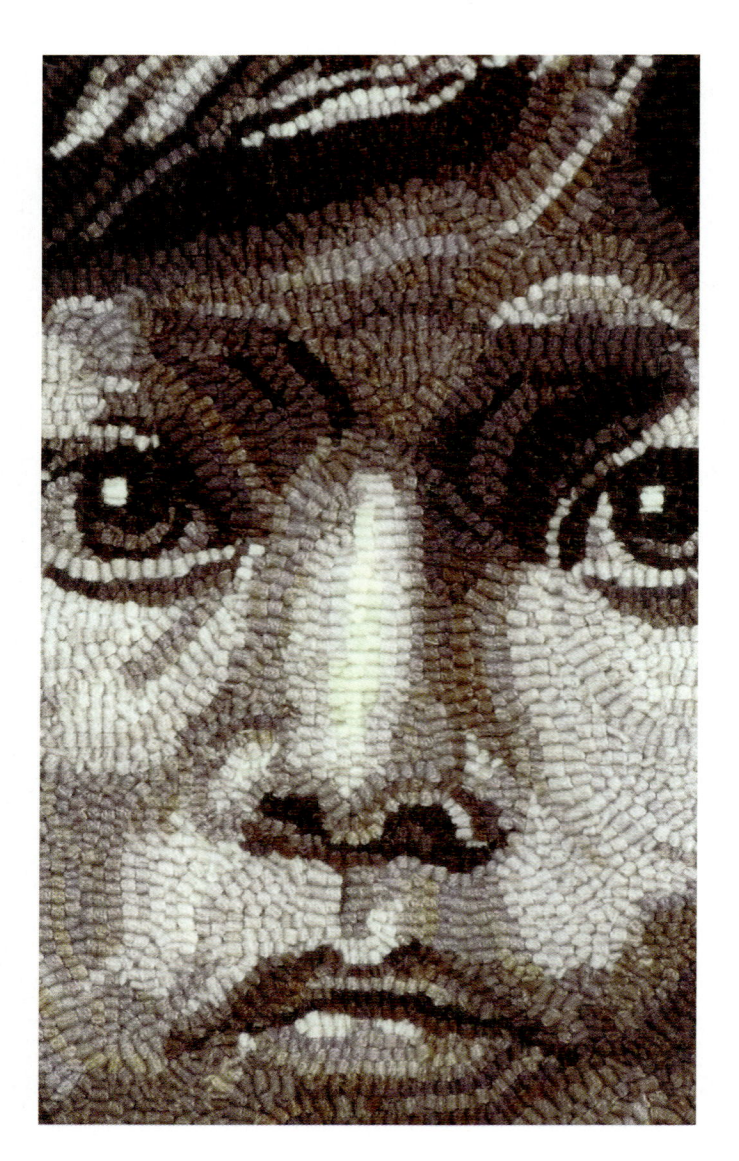

In the Judges' Words

- *Wonderful monochromatic facial features. Highlights and shadows make facial expression endearing.*
- *Movement in the background is perfect.*
- *Use of purple in a neutral palette is brilliant.*
- *The simple beaded-line border is just right to set off the subject.*

Donna K. Hrkman
Dayton, Ohio

Donna started out hooking primitive cuts and styles about 10 years ago but has since embraced fine cuts. As a full-time artist, she sells and exhibits her rugs, takes commissions, and has a standing display at a local art gallery. Over the past 10 years, this ATHA and Green Mountain Rug Hooking Guild member has hooked more than 100 rugs. Indian Boy—Ah-Chee-Lo is her fifth rug to be featured in Celebration.

Indian Boy—Ah-Chee-Lo, 28″ x 33″, #3-cut hand-dyed wool on cotton linen backing. Adapted from a photograph by Edward Curtis and hooked by Donna Hrkman, Dayton, Ohio, 2011.

ADAPTATION DESIGNS

La Japonaise

Karen Whidden's current inspirations for hooking rugs come from master Impressionist painters. Her intricate depiction of a Japanese woman dressed in traditional garb and surrounded by fans is an adaptation of Claude Monet's work by the same name.

While some artists might be deterred by researching the history of a source of inspiration, Karen finds that the additional information feeds into her understanding of the original painting and helps her to create a rug that is as true as possible to the original source.

"I researched as many images and adaptations of *La Japonaise* as I could find and used the colors I felt best captured the sentiment of the original painting," she said. "In researching the painting and the artist I discovered that the subject was, in fact, Claude Monet's wife, Camille."

Karen dyed all new wool for this rug. She used straight, spot, and overdyeing techniques. The wall in the background is Dorr's teal wool spot dyed with Pro Chem navy, evergreen, bright, and yellow in both light and dark shades and then blended to create variation on the wall. Pro Chem's Chinese Red over natural wool with spots of bright red and black give the robe the rich appearance of silk.

Karen points to the robe as the most difficult part of hooking this design. She found help in a technique described by Eric Sandberg in *Celebration* X. "By turning the piece upside down and hooking individual sections he was able to successfully capture lights, darks, and highlights. I found that using this method made hooking *La Japonaise* fun and less stressful."

In the Judges' Words

- Beautiful work and detail—a more vibrant version of the Monet painting.
- Detail in rug, fans, and gown are well executed.
- Extraordinary painting, and this hooker has done it justice.
- The face, usually so difficult, is exquisite.

Karen Whidden
Southern Pines, North Carolina

Karen completed three latch hook kits before she purchased wool, a cutter, dyes, and rug warp in 2003. Since then she has hooked over 125 pieces, including rugs, pillows, mats, and wall hangings. She finds rug hooking to be creative and relaxing and does most of her hooking in the evening while watching television with her husband. La Japonaise is Karen's fifth rug to appear in Celebration. She is a member of McGown, ATHA, and the Sandhills Rug Artists, and her work is exhibited and sold at The Artist Gallery in Southern Pines.

La Japonaise, 24" x 40", #3-, 4-, and 5-cut wool on rug warp.
Adapted from a Claude Monet 1876 painting and hooked by Karen Whidden, Southern Pines, North Carolina, 2010.

ADAPTATION DESIGNS

Lake Shore

Roland Nunn's goal in hooking this rug was to capture the serenity he saw in an unlabeled photograph of this beautiful lakeside scene. The picture is from an often-photographed vista in Pictured Rocks National Lakeshore (National Park) on Lake Superior in Upper Michigan.

"I particularly liked the reflections in the water combined with a different part of the shoreline shown through the hole in the rock formation," Roland says. The positioning of the rocks forms a natural frame around the island in the distance.

The combination of the rocky outcropping and the smooth water made a vivid contrast that Roland found challenging to hook. He worked hard to show the texture in the curving formation of the stone

Roland notes that the choice of swatches is the most important part of hooking a landscape. Because of that, he dyes all of his own wool and works mostly in swatches. For *Lake Shore* he used 29 different swatches. The large number was necessitated by the changing colors in the rocks and their reflections, the variety of blues in the water and the sky, and the greens in the trees on the island. "The use of a parent (base) swatch plus its transitional companions allows for subtle variations in color with smooth transitions."

Lake Shore, 35" x 38", #3-cut on monk's cloth.
Adapted from a photograph of unknown origin and hooked by Roland Nunn, Orinda, California, 2011.

In the Judges' Words

- Wonderful use of dimension giving the 3-D effect to the picture.
- Realistic use of colors.
- Great show of reflections in the water.
- Dark, medium, light, and bright give a sense of distance and closeness.

ROLAND C. NUNN
ORINDA, CALIFORNIA

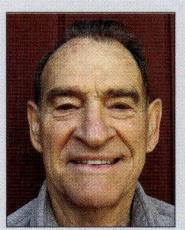

Roland started rug hooking 22 years ago at age 60 when he found that he needed a "sit-down" hobby. To date he has hooked 61 pieces in a number of styles, including geometric, oriental, floral, animals, landscapes, and scrolls. He has attended the McGown conference at Asilomar in Pacific Grove, California, for 15 years and taught 2 of his granddaughters how to hook. Lake Shore is his seventh rug to be featured in Celebration.

ADAPTATION DESIGNS

Ram Tough

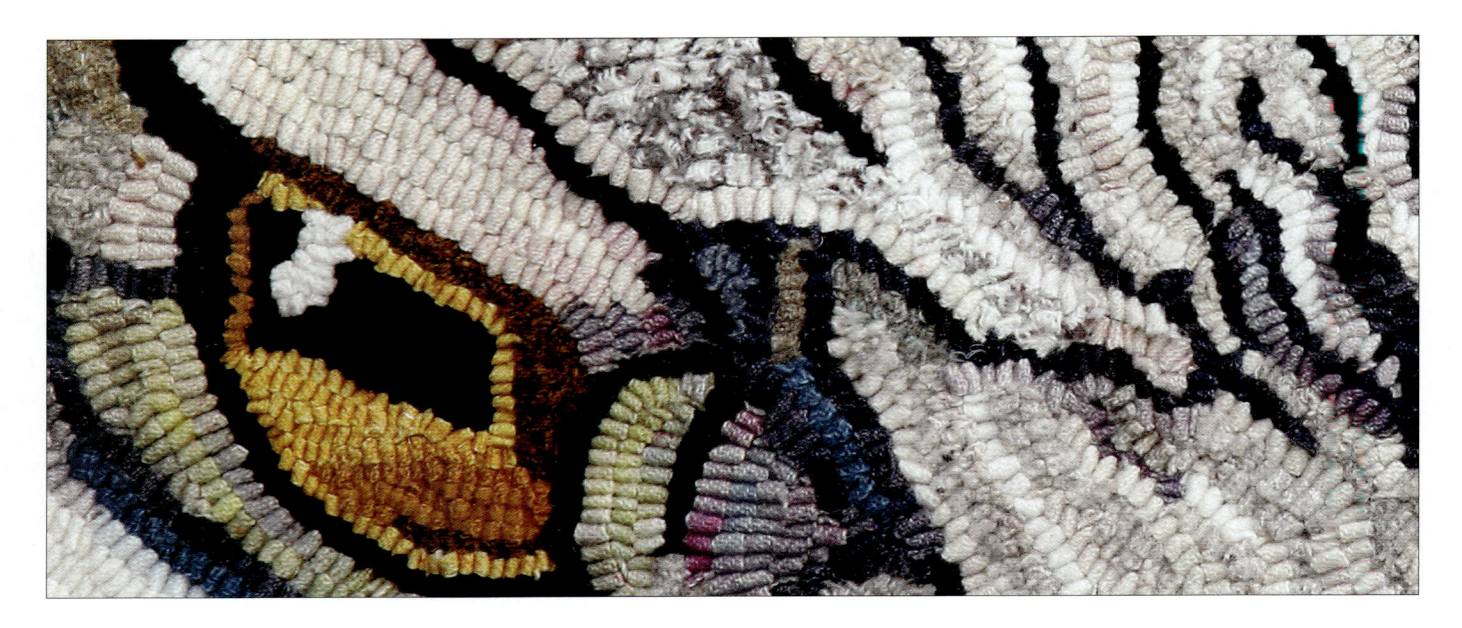

Take a good look at the eyes that Michele Wise hooked into this rug. There is no doubt that this is one tough ram.

Those eyes are Michele's favorite part of this rug. "The eyes draw one into the rug. They are the brightest and lightest part and make the animal look fierce," she said.

Ram Tough is an adaptation of a Pendleton Woolen Mills poster that Michele saw at a local fair. The ram's eyes caught her attention as she was finishing up a rug hooking demonstration. After drawing a pattern from a photograph, she contacted Pendleton for permission to recreate the ram in wool.

Michele used recycled, textured, and natural wool, dyeing with a number of techniques including overdyeing, abrash, and casserole. She also used as-is wool, especially in the background.

In hooking such a symmetrical design, Michele had to concentrate on working both sides of the ram's face consistently. "I always had to look at the other side to see if I was interpreting it in the same way. I used the higgledy-piggledy method of hooking the fleece to add more texture; one has to be careful to make the wool flat in the back and fill in all the spaces."

Michele also challenged herself to use uncommon colors in the rug. "Getting the horns to stand out and be shaded with different-colored wool was a fun challenge."

Ram Tough won Reserved Grand Champion at the Western Washington State Fair and was named one of the Viewers' Choice rugs at the 2011 Green Mountain rug show.

In the Judges' Words

- *Amazing detail in a wide cut. Beautifully executed.*
- *A visually exciting and strong piece. Well interpreted into rug hooking.*
- *The eyes show the fierceness of the ram. It has a cold and menacing feeling.*
- *Finishing is beautiful. Good color rendition.*

MICHELE WISE
SEABECK, WASHINGTON

Michele Wise has hooked more than 100 rugs in the past 12 years. An avid quilter who loves all things handworked, she started rug hooking after taking an introductory course. At that time she had never seen rug hooking done. Michele is a McGown certified teacher, current director of the Western McGown workshop, and co-director of Puget Sound Rug Show. In addition to rugs, she enjoys applying rug hooking to three-dimensional objects, including dolls, furniture, cupboard doors, and books.

Ram Tough, 108" x 160", #6-, 7-, and 8-cut new and recycled wool on linen. Adapted from a Pendleton poster (with permission) and hooked by Michele Wise, Seabeck, Washington, 2011. ALL THINGS PHOTOGRAPHY/AMY PHEASANT

ADAPTATION DESIGNS

Southern Leopard Frog and Tri-colored Heron

Judy Carter is continually looking for ways to stretch and improve and push the limits of what can be achieved with a hook and wool. When she saw Carel Pieter Brest van Kempen's painting, her first thought was, "Could I hook this?"

The viewer seems to be at the bottom of the pond, looking up as a frog dives down and away from a hungry heron that is hovering above and is distorted by the surface of the water. "I loved the colors and the unique underwater perspective," she says. "I couldn't stop thinking about it."

Judy dyed 6- and 8-value swatches in an open pot method so she could dye a large quantity of new wool at a time. "Carel planned the colors," she says. "I duplicated them by dyeing my wool to match his painting." Plastic beads portray the bubbles.

What Judy thought would be the simplest part of the hooking process—the ripples—turned out to be her biggest challenge. "I thought they would be the easiest and best part because they are so colorful, but it was a challenge to get the colors and values in the right places."

Judy's favorite part of the finished rug is the colorful frog that draws the viewer's first glance. It isn't until the viewer looks deeper and discovers the heron's threat that the frog's plight is truly understood. "I love how he looks like he really is diving and getting away from the heron," she says.

To finish the rug, Judy basted cording under the backing and whipped the edges with yarn as she attached one side of the rug tape. It hangs in a hallway where the morning light makes the beads sparkle.

In the Judges' Words
- Captured the movement of both the details and the background.
- The ebb, flow, and whirl of the water make it work.
- Use of embellishment to execute bubbles is great.
- Loved the shadow of the heron.

Judy Carter
Willow Street, Pennsylvania

Judy took a beginning rug hooking class from Pat Moyer in 1993 simply because it would be "fun to learn something new." She finished her 100th rug on December 31, 2011. She enjoys hooking close-up portraits of animals but will choose any pattern that challenges her. Judy is a branch manager for a credit union, president of the Northern McGown Teachers Workshop, and an ATHA member. This piece is her ninth to be chosen for Celebration.

Southern Leopard Frog and Tri-colored Heron, *38" x 26", #3-, 4-, and 8-cut. Adapted from a painting by Carel Pieter Brest van Kempen (with permission) and hooked by Judy Carter, Willow Street, Pennsylvania, 2010.*

ADAPTATION DESIGNS

Sylvia

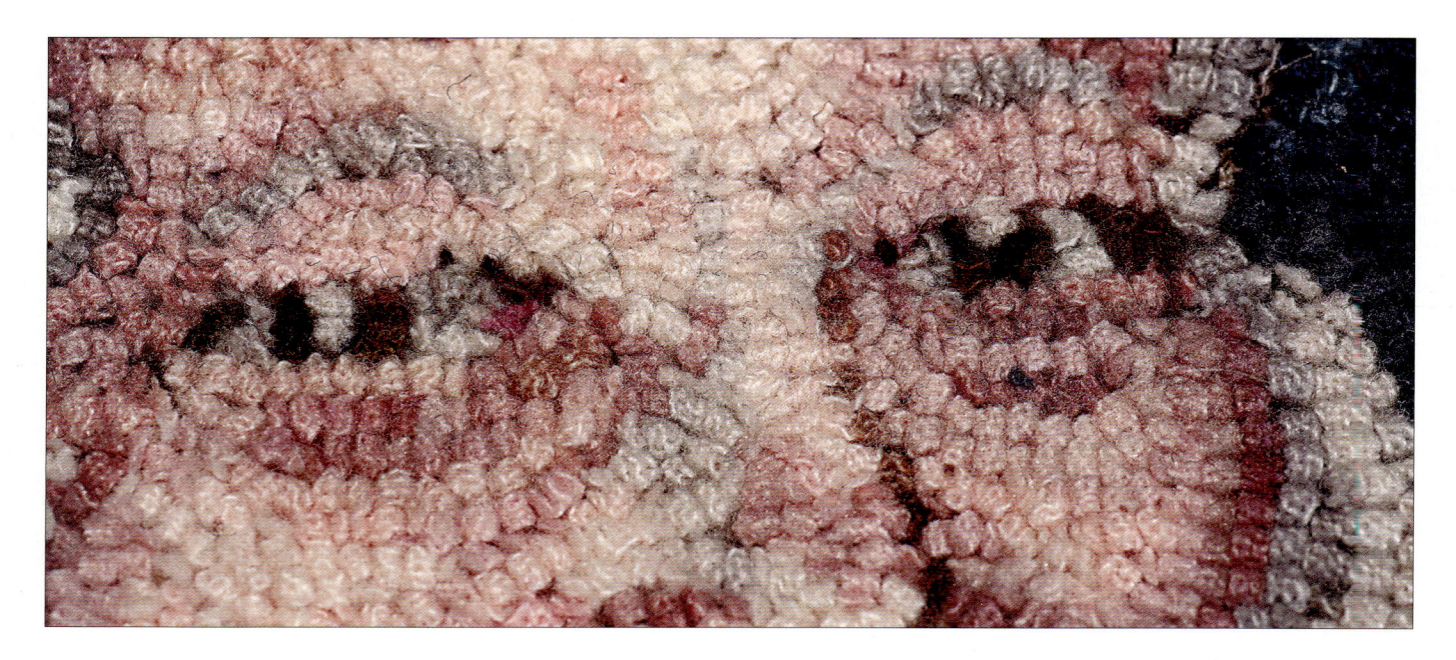

The challenges of hooking a portrait of someone you know—and who will be the recipient of the finished piece—are enormous as Kay Bowman found out in making this hooked portrait of her friend Sylvia. "My challenge was to capture Sylvia's personality," she says. "I knew that I could not present this gift unless it really looked like her."

Kay chose to adapt a photo that had been taken years earlier by Sylvia's late husband. Because she only had three weeks until Sylvia's ninetieth birthday party, Kay pulled as much of the wool as she could from her stash. "Sometimes less is more," she says. "The challenge of using only the wool I had on hand was at times frustrating, but in the end, it was a satisfying feeling of accomplishment."

The flesh tones and tints that Kay used in Sylvia's face had been dyed using the paintbrush method. She chose spot-dyed wool for the background, and wool from a gradated swatch and spot dyes worked well for the hair. The only wool Kay needed to dye was the magenta of Sylvia's sweater. She added a bit of Lopi yarn in the hair.

Kay's favorite part of the portrait is Sylvia's smile. "She smiles with her eyes as well as her mouth," she says

Kay added several rows of hooking all the way around the portrait, wrapped the hooking over a wooden frame, and covered the back with a piece of dyed magenta wool.

Of course, there was just one little tweak after the fact when Kay discovered a four-loop, odd-colored patch on the neck in Sylvia's portrait. She undid just enough of the stitching on the backing to remove and replace the offending loops.

In the Judges' Words

- *Very good adaption of snapshot to rug hooking.*
- *Background—good choice to place the subject in the foreground.*
- *Skin tone color is wonderful.*
- *A really well done portrait (especially the teeth!).*

Kay Bowman
New Glasgow, Nova Scotia, Canada

Kay always anticipated learning to hook and had quite a supply of woolen skirts, sweaters, yarns, and blankets in waiting. When the local school board sponsored a rug hooking course, she enrolled immediately. Her teacher, Sylvia Macdonald, is the subject of this rug. Kay enjoys hooking primitive styles and likes to incorporate textures such as fleece, yarns, and novelty fibers. She belongs to the Rug Hooking Guild of Nova Scotia. This rug is her second to be featured in Celebration.

Sylvia, 8½" x 11½", #3-cut dyed wool on monk's cloth. Adapted from a family photograph and hooked by Kay Bowman, New Glasgow, Nova Scotia, Canada, 2011.

ADAPTATION DESIGNS

The Beauty of Keith Richards

Mischelle Page Hodgkin admits to a love/hate relationship when it comes to designing, but because of her obsession with rug hooking and the joy she gets from creating, she more often than not opts to design her own rugs. For this portrait of Rolling Stones guitarist Keith Richards, Mischelle worked from royalty free stock photos.

Mischelle discovered that she liked the challenge of hooking portraits after she took a class on hooking faces with Diane Phillips. She chose to turn her creative skills to painting Keith Richards in wool for a camp project with rug hooking instructor Gail Dufresne.

"My project choice was the face of Keith Richards as I wanted the face to have character," she says. "I wasn't sure it would work out but I was more than pleased with the result."

Mischelle did not color plan her project in advance. Gail chose the signature red for the headband and the project moved forward from there. Mischelle used spot and other dye techniques on new and recycled wool to finish the project. At Gail's encouragement, she often included colors that seemed rather bold for a portrait. Blues, purples, and greens are mixed in with the browns of the hair, and a variety of pastels create the contours of the face.

Mischelle's love/hate outlook on designing filtered into the creative process as well when she started on the lips. That part of the rug was both exciting and frustrating. "Those lips are my favorite as they were reworked about 50 times. They were challenging; I just kept at it."

The final piece is professionally framed and hangs over the fireplace in her bedroom.

In the Judges' Words

- *Captured the personality.*
- *Essence of the subject is shown through the eyes and pose.*
- *A tough, gutsy piece of rug hooking.*
- *A creative portrait that really "gets" the subject and stretches the envelope in a good way.*

The Beauty of Keith Richards, 18" x 20", #3- and 6-cut dyed wool on linen. Adapted from royalty-free photographs and hooked by Mischelle Page Hodgkin, Winchester, Kentucky, 2011. SPECTRUM PHOTOGRAPHY

Mischelle Page Hodgkin
Winchester, Kentucky

Mischelle and her husband obtained their US Coast Guard Captain licenses and for 15 years ran a motor yacht in the waters near the Bahamas, the United States, Cuba, and Mexico. A friend introduced Mischelle to rug hooking about 12 years ago and since then she's discovered that pillows are her favorite items to hook. She is a member of ATHA, the Winchester Art Guild, and the Kentucky Guild of Artists and Craftsmen. Her inclusion in Celebration is her first rug hooking award.

ADAPTATION DESIGNS

Turtle Reflection

Jon Ciemiewicz started this rug hooking project with a sea lion in mind but ended up with a sea turtle instead. "I was on the Web looking for a good sea lion pattern to hook and had found one by Thomas Vignaud," he said. "As I looked through his website, the photograph of a turtle with its reflection on the surface of the water looked like the kind of challenge that I enjoy."

Jon color planned and dyed all new Dorr wool for this intriguing point-of-view design. He used a spot dye for the turtle's shell and mottled colors for the rest of the elements.

While the realistic turtle—from its expression to the patterns on its shell—proved fun to hook, Jon found himself faced with a lot of hooking and re-hooking when he tried to tackle the reflected and distorted images that surrounded the swimming turtle.

"The real challenge was in getting the distorted reflection of the turtle on the surface of the water and again the distorted palm trees as seen through the water to look realistic," he said.

Jon needed about three months to complete the rug. He mounted it on artist stretcher bars and it is currently hanging in the guest bathroom of his house. Jon got closer to mastering patience through his work on this rug. "Do not get frustrated if it does not come out just as you would like the first time," he says. "Take out the strips that you don't like and fix it."

In the Judges' Words

- Turtle shows movement in the water.
- Good use of color and execution of detail.
- Hooking is immaculate.
- Beautifully executed and finished.

Jon Ciemiewicz
Hudson, New Hampshire

Jon tried many fiber arts with the idea of focusing on just one during his retirement. It wasn't until a 5-minute lesson at the Dorr Mill Store that he knew that rug hooking was the hobby he'd been searching for. Over the ensuing 16 years he estimates he has hooked about 40 rugs. He prefers #3 and 4 cuts and scenes that involve wild animals or Native Americans. Jon is a member in numerous guilds. His work his been chosen for Celebration several times.

Turtle Reflection, 20" x 25", #4-cut hand-dyed wool on linen. Adapted from a photograph by Thomas Vignaud (with permission) and hooked by Jon Ciemiewicz, Hudson, New Hampshire, 2011.

GeneShepherd.com

The Internet Rug Camp
Cambria Pines Rug Camp

Bent Hooks, Specialty Wool, DVDs

www.geneshepherd.com gene@geneshepherd.com

Ault's Rug Hooking Store
NOW SHIPPING

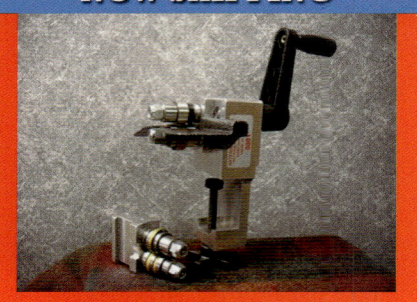

Ault's Wool Fabric Cutting Machine and Ault's Universal Cutterheads

Our machine and cutterheads are easy to use. Just drop in the cutterhead and start cutting hooked strips from size 4 through size 10. This is a clamp on machine.

Ault's Rug Hooking Store
49 East Main Street
Shelby, OH 44875

(866) 659-1752 (toll-free)
Larry.Ault@gmail.com
www.Aults.com

Hooked in the Mountains XVI

Hooked Rug and Fiber Art Exhibit
of the Green Mt. Rug Hooking Guild

November 10-17, 2012

At the Shelburne Museum's Round Barn, Shelburne, Vermont

Featuring the Art of Ann Winterling Catherine Henning and Elizabeth Guth

- Over 450 Works of Hooked Art
- More than 20 Vendors

3 Day Workshops held throughout the 8-day show. Teachers this year include:

Liz Alpert Fay	Sara Judith
Rae Harrell	Diane Learmonth
Anne-Marie Littenberg	Diane Burgess
Lisanne Miller	Judy Carter
Janet Conner	Donna Hrkman
Judith Dallegret	Diane Phillips

Artist's Reception
Guest Speakers Daily
Children's Education Programs
Special Package Tours
Silent Auction
Raffle Rug
Refreshments

For more information please visit
www.gmrhg.org
802-434-8191

Show Hours: 10 am–5 pm daily • $8 adults, $6 seniors, children under 12 are Free. $15 weeklong passes.

LAP HOOPS

Rug Hooking Lap Frame with Gripper Strips

Original Lap Hoop

All Wood Design

- Ingenious pivot & swivel design allows your work to rotate 360° while the base remains steady in your lap.
- Cross bar adds extra strength as well as providing an arm rest to help minimize fatigue.
- Recently awarded by Chiropractors and endorsed by "Hooked on Rugs."

Gruber's Quilt Shop

Visit us for all your rug hooking & quilting needs!

1.877.778.7793
or **320.259.4360**

Located in the Dantree Court
310 4th Ave NE • Waite Park, MN 56387
www.grubersquiltshop.com

SHOWCASE OF
Primitive Designs

PRIMITIVE

A rug that is simple in design, materials, and technique. Primitive rugs usually use wider cuts, and are naive or simple in design with little or no shading, exaggerated scale, or unrealistic proportion.

PRIMITIVE DESIGNS
Animal Crackers

Each year Gail Ferdinando meets her stepmother and her sister at the Marriott Residence Inn in Princeton, New Jersey, for a long weekend of rug hooking. Last year's challenge was to design a primitive style rug using primitive colors. "I like simple designs without a lot of distraction," she says, "and knew I could add some interest with hooking. I chose a runner because I had the perfect spot for it in my house."

Gail pulled from her stash of soft primitive colors when color planning this rug. She was especially interested in using the muted golds, browns, reds, and grays that are traditionally used in primitive style rugs. She chose mostly new wool, some recycled wool, and a small bit of paisley.

When it comes to picking one favorite motif, Gail admits to having a hard time. "The tiger is one of my favorite parts of the rug," she says. "He is the first thing I hooked into the rug, and before he was halfway done, I knew the rug would work." She also likes the way the background hooked up. "I had no plan and just kind of made it up as I went along. Even though it's pretty simple, I was so happy at how well it worked."

Gail is taken with the border, even though the border that she likes so much proved to be the most challenging part of the rug. "I had some ideas in mind and tried a few, but nothing was working," she says. "I looked at some antique rugs for inspiration and came up with something simple that worked perfectly."

Gail Ferdinando
Pittstown, New Jersey

When Gail and her sister showed an interest in rug hooking, Gail's stepmom made beginner kits for each of the girls. They started on a Friday, finished on a Sunday, and went out later that same day to buy a bigger pattern and more wool. As an adult, Gail has been hooking rugs as a serious pastime for about 12 years and has completed 25 rugs. She is a member of several rug hooking guilds. This rug marks her first win in Celebration.

In the Judges' Words

- *Like the way the border holds everything in.*
- *Very partial to the patchwork animals, especially the cat.*
- *Liked the use of one color to create the animals.*
- *Well done primitive, both in color and design.*

Animal Crackers, 22 1/2" x 61", #8- and 8 1/2-cut wool and paisley on linen. Designed and hooked by Gail Ferdinando, Pittstown, New Jersey, 2011.

PRIMITIVE DESIGNS

Distelfink

In a crunch to find a pattern for a rug camp she was attending, Cynthia Norwood called pattern designer Barbara Carroll to ask what she had available. Barbara found this pattern of a distelfink, a motif from Pennsylvania Dutch folk art, and Cynthia's mind immediately began to color plan.

Cynthia enjoys working antique paisley into her rugs and started with that in mind when she color planned the rug. "I could see where antique paisley would be used perfectly," she says. With Barbara's help, the two planned the rug to show off not just pieces of antique paisley shawls, but also to incorporate textured wools directly off the bolt. "I used four different fabrics," she says, "but one was a great plaid so it looks as if I used many more fabrics."

To this day, Cynthia is still amazed by the background of the rug. "It makes the rest of the rug sing," she says. "The bird and flowers are a higher chroma than I normally use, and the dark background made them even stronger."

Another amazing tidbit about this rug is that Cynthia can't identify any challenges other than the stress of thinking that she had no pattern for the upcoming camp. "Some rugs just fall completely into place," she says. "This was one of those rugs. It sort of hooked itself!"

Cynthia finished this rug with wool fabric, a look she likes for primitive rugs more than an edge whipped with yarn.

In hooking this rug, Cynthia learned that preplanning, which is always suggested, isn't always necessary. "Sometimes showing up without a plan is the best action," she says.

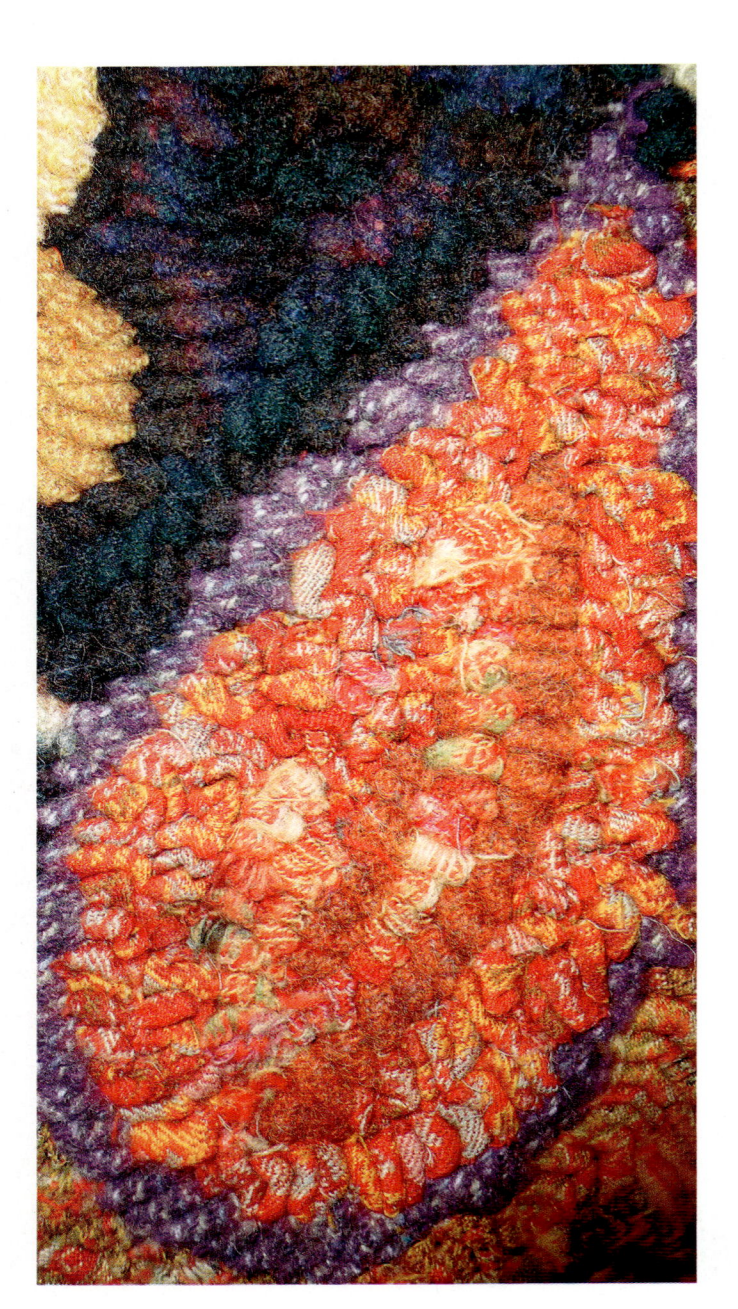

In the Judges' Words

- Like the mix of paisley and other wool, the richness of the colors and combinations.
- Nicely done wide cut.
- Great choice of background.
- Nice finish with wool binding.

CYNTHIA NORWOOD
AUSTIN, TEXAS

Cynthia had never seen a hooked rug until she moved to northeast Ohio in 1980 and went to the state's Apple Butter Festival. Since then she estimates that she has hooked a couple hundred pieces. She enjoys working with very large strips and pieces from antique paisley shawls. She is a McGown certified teacher and runs and teaches rug camps across the country. This rug is her fifth to be chosen for Celebration.

Distelfink, 25" x 21", 9 mm-cut wool and paisley on linen.
Pattern by Barbara Carroll; hooked by Cynthia Norwood, Austin, Texas, 2011.

PRIMITIVE DESIGNS

Four and Twenty Blackbirds

Wendy Powell appreciates the storytelling aspect of rug hooking. "I like to put several borders around the 'story,'" she says, "to not only capture the story but also to create additional design and warmth in the rug and to frame the essence of the rug."

That's the exact approach she took when designing this primitive rug. "I have always loved the primitive look of blackbirds and crows," she says. "And I wanted to have four (birds in the pie) and twenty (on the border) to express the nursery rhyme."

Wendy color planned her rug so the colors would reflect the timelessness and "old age" of the nursery rhyme. She purchased new and recycled wool, some of it dyed, while keeping in mind that everything in the rug needed to look aged.

Her favorite part of the rug is the blackbirds in the border. "They all have different personalities," she said, "and they frame the theme of the rug."

Her biggest challenge was positioning the birds in the pie to look like they were singing. "I finally put light blue wool around them," she says, "and the pie seemed to define them better and made them stand out more."

Wendy finished the rug with yarn and finishing tape. In hooking this rug she became more aware of the function that borders play in rug hooking. "I learned the importance of borders in a finished rug. I like that it makes the subject or essence of the rug feel cozy and important. The completed rug is displayed, appropriately so, in her dining room.

In the Judges' Words

- A clever original design, balanced and active, detailed, and with a real sense of humor.
- Great lettering.
- Excellent border design.

WENDY POWELL
SANTA YNEZ, CALIFORNIA

Wendy's grandmother was a rug hooker and she grew up with all sorts of rugs in her house. The one she remembers most is the stair runner that tells the story of her grandmother's life. So when she had the opportunity in 2004 to take rug hooking lessons, she jumped at the chance. She has hooked 30 rugs to date. This is her second rug to be included in Celebration.

Four and Twenty Blackbirds, 41" x 30", #6- and 8-cut wool on monk's cloth.
Designed and hooked by Wendy Powell, Santa Ynez, California, 2011. BILL DEWEY

PRIMITIVE DESIGNS

Yankee Ingenuity

"Use it up, wear it out, make it do, or do without" was Teresa Heinze's mantra as she hooked this rug. And by the time she got to the last prodded strip, she had only a handful of wool left. "This is exactly what the hookers of that time did," she says.

This pattern, offered as a class by June Mikoryak, is an exact copy of an antique rug from around the late 1800s to early 1900s. The formal motif in the center was taken from Persian rugs—a style that many women admired but couldn't afford and so duplicated it in their own creations—and the primitive flowers in the corners used the same colors as the center.

As part of the class, June planned the colors for each student so that no two rugs would look alike. For Teresa's rug, she chose over-dyed herringbones, tweeds, and other textures plus some new wool and some recycled clothing. Teresa's favorite part of the rug is how all these different textures work together to give the rug interest.

For Teresa, the most challenging part of hooking the rug was hooking the horizontal lines in the background. To help, June divided the rug into thirds. A set of diagonal lines was drawn to hook the short, colored stripes so they would be even on each side of the center motif.

Teresa learned to hook a proddy edge to finish the rug. One row of reverse hooking followed by three rows of proddy meant that no whipping or rug binding was needed.

In the Judges' Words

- Comfortable, analogous color scheme.
- There is a boldness and a simplicity to this rug that I really appreciate.
- The directional hooking adds to the strength of the design; the creative use of beading to contain the elements holds it together; and the fringed edge is a playful icing on the top.

TERESA HEINZE
LUBBOCK, TEXAS

In 1996, Teresa purchased a small rug kit for Little White Dog. *Between the directions in the box and the help of daily phone calls to friend Delores McGlashon, Teresa finished her first hooked rug. She has finished more than 60 in the years since. Teresa started Hub City Rughookers in 2001 and is a member of ATHA.* Yankee Ingenuity *is her first rug to be chosen for* Celebration.

Yankee Ingenuity, 34" x 21", #5-, 6-, 8-, and 10-cut wool on Scottish linen.
Pattern by June Mikoryak; hooked by Teresa Heinze, Lubbock, Texas, 2011. NAOMI HILL

RUG HOOKING MARKETPLACE

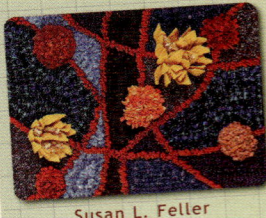

Design Basics for Rug Hookers
In *Design Basics for Rug Hookers*, author Susan Feller walks you through the basics a rug hooker should know about rug design. She provides a wealth of knowledge and guidance for beginning and intermediate hookers, and it's a wonderful refresher for the seasoned hooker. From the design elements every hooker should know to how to develop an appealing design, lessons on color and contrast, balance and movement, texture and patterning, *Design Basics* covers it all. It's the perfect resource for anyone designing a work of art in wool. **Price: $24.95***

Rugs in Bloom
Shading flowers can be daunting, whether it is for a fine-cut project or one that is primitive. With *Rugs in Bloom*, you'll find clear, concise directions on how to "paint" flowers with wool. Let author Jane Halliwell Green guide you through techniques for shading using her easy-to-follow diagrams. The author gives instructions on how to hook more than 40 different flowers. Jane includes several signature dye recipes and a stunning FREE pull-out pattern. *Rugs in Bloom* is an essential resource for anyone who wishes to learn or improve on their shading techniques for nature's most beautiful gift, the flower. **Price: $29.95***

Hooked Portraits
Hooking the human face or capturing the personality of your favorite pet can be intimidating. Why not let well-known author and fiber artist Anne-Marie Littenberg walk you through the challenges and teach you the intricacies of how to hook a rug portrait? You'll learn to design classic head shots and figures, to create profiles or front views, and better understand the art of the self-portrait. This book is full of tips and tricks for adding depth, dimension, and emotions through shading and lines and it is the definitive guide for creating portraits in wool. Whether you are interested in hooking a member of your family, the family pet, or someone you admire, author Anne-Marie Littenberg will teach you the tips and techniques for achieving the look you are after. **Price: $29.95***

Geometric Hooked Rugs
Geometric Hooked Rugs, written by rug hooking teacher, artist, and designer Gail Dufresne, demystifies hooking geometric rugs. Gail describes her signature look of superimposing figures on top of complex geometric backgrounds. Geometric hooked rugs may look simple, but they are a challenge to do well. This book explains the elements and principles of design, including balance and unity, repetition, proportion, and movement. Learn to color plan a geometric rug, including how to use color values effectively. Plus, you'll learn tips and techniques for dyeing the wool, finishing the rug, and designing your own geometric patterns. **Price: $24.95***

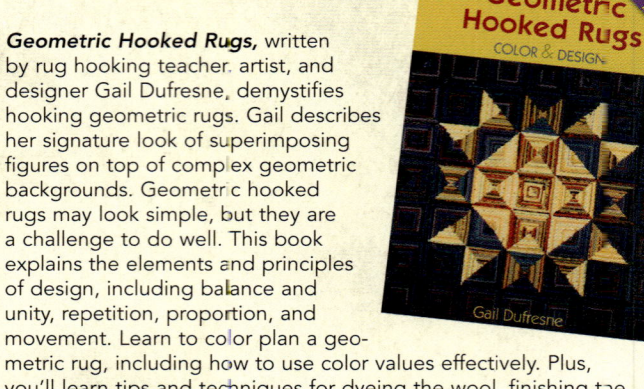

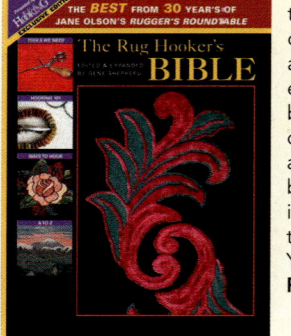

The Rug Hooker's Bible
For over 30 years, Jane Olson taught rug hooking to rug hookers of all levels—beginners to advanced. Now this collaborative effort with Gene Shepherd has become a classic for rug hookers—a clear, concise "Bible" for the novice as well as the seasoned hooker. This beautifully illustrated book, written in an easy-to-read format, will open the door to the art of rug hooking. You won't want to be without it! **Price: $29.95***

Learn At Home DVD Series
For even more help and guidance with rug hooking, we invite you to purchase the **"Learn at Home DVD Series"** with your teacher Gene Shepherd. See different methods in intricate detail, repeat sections at the push of a button (as often as you wish), or freeze-frame any section for as long as you need. These DVDs are designed as an instructional addition to Chapters 2 and 3 of *The Rug Hooker's Bible*. Bring hooking lessons into the comfort of your home! DVD Vol. 1 (Hooking 101) and DVD Vol. 2 (Multiple Ways to Hook). **Price: $17.95 per DVD or $35.90 for both***

You don't want to be without these informative books. Order today!

*Plus shipping & handling

To order any or all of these items, visit us online @ www.rughookingmagazine.com OR call us toll-free: 1-877-462-2604 (US & Canada).

SHOWCASE OF
Honorable Mention

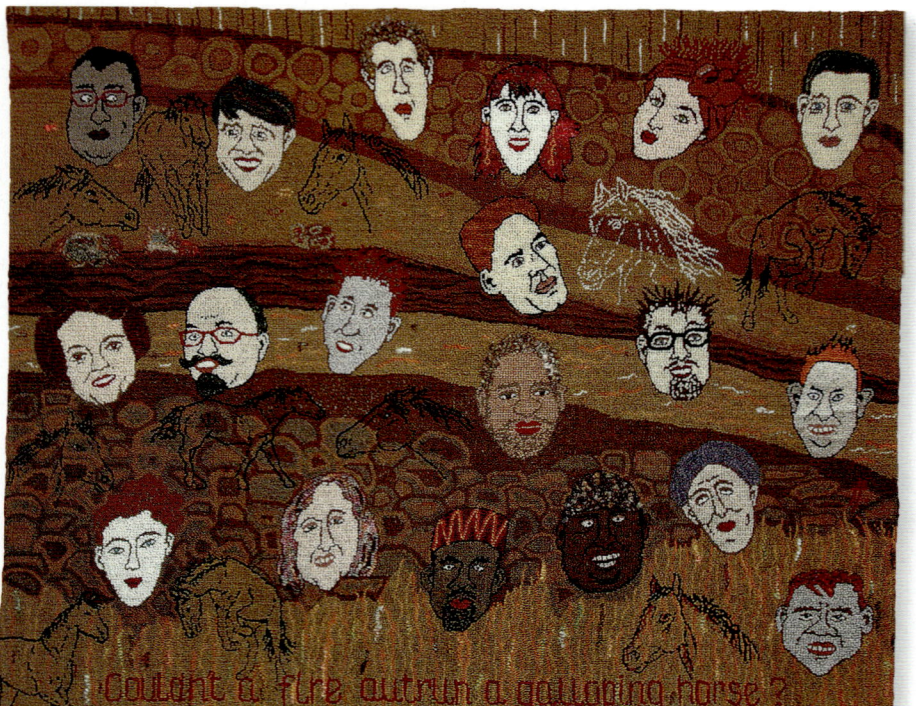

Couldn't a Fire Outrun a Galloping Horse?, 63" x 52", alpaca, silk, wool yarn, and #6- and 8-cut wool on Scottish burlap. Designed and hooked by Halina Bienkowski, Amherst, Nova Scotia, Canada, 2010.

Flight, 26" x 23½", #4-cut Dorr wool on linen. Designed and hooked by Liz Marino, South Egremont, Massachusetts, 2011. JANE MCWHORTER

Sable Island Horse No. 1, 37" x 36", #3-cut Dorr wool, various Fleece Artist and other yarns, and roving on linen. Designed and hooked by Suzanne Gunn, Centreville, Nova Scotia, Canada, 2011.

Alamo Garden, 35½" x 25", #3-cut wool on rug warp. Designed and hooked by Phyllis Mulligan, Swannanoa, North Carolina, 2011. KYM DRUM PHOTOGRAPHY

Beauty and the Beast, 27½" x 41½", #3- and 4-cut wool, decorative ribbon for gems and tears on monk's cloth. Designed and hooked by Katy Powell, Portland, Oregon, 2011. OWEN CAREY

My Labs, 24½" x 17", #3-cut Dorr wool on linen. Designed and hooked by Chizuko Hayami, Setagaya, Tokyo, Japan, 2010.

Palazzo Di Piero, 54" x 78", hand-cut wool on linen. Designed and hooked by Janet T. Conner, Hiram, Maine, 2010.
ANNE LEVINE AND RACHAEL CONNER

Somewhere Over the Bakken (in the Badlands of ND), 46½" x 34", #8-, 8½-, and 9-cut recycled as-is and new dyed wool, and wool yarn on linen. Designed and hooked by Carolyn Godfread, Bismark, North Dakota, 2011. D'JOYCE PHOTOGRAPHE

Halloween Hooligans, 34" x 26", various cuts of wool, wool roving, and buttons on linen. Pattern by Maria Barton; hooked by Natasha Chan, Carmel, Indiana, 2011.

SPRUCE RIDGE STUDIOS 
Kris Miller
1786 Eager Rd.
Howell, MI 48855
(517) 546-7732
kris@spruceridgestudios.com

Delightful original primitive rug hooking patterns and supplies
Mail order or by appointment

www.spruceridgestudios.com

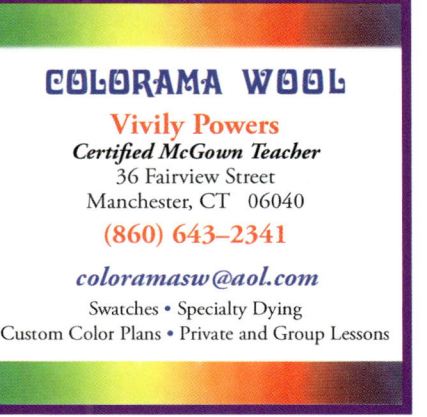

GREEN MOUNTAIN HOOKED RUGS
Wool
Supplies
Classes
Hook-ins
Online Store

GREEN MOUNTAIN RUG SCHOOL
In June ~ VT Technical College

FALL FOLIAGE FIESTA
In Sept ~ VT College of Fine Arts

2838 County Rd, Montpelier, VT 05602
802-223-1333
GreenMountainHookedRugs.com

"Everybody Needs Fiber." — Susan Feller

www.RuckmanMillFarm.com

2012 Selected One of America's Best & Listed in The Directory of Traditional American Crafts — Early American Life magazine

Design Basics for Rug Hookers — Susan L. Feller

Shop On-Line Anytime
Patterns Book
Workshops ArtWools
Design in A Box

DESIGN IN A BOX — Frakturs — CREATE YOUR OWN FOLK ART PATTERN WITH

Ruckman Mill Farm
PO Box 409
Augusta, WV 26704
304-496-8073
rugs2wv@yahoo.com

www.ArtWools.com

Painted Mermaid Designs
by artist Brenda Ellis Sauro

Patterns
Commissions
Classes

Colorful Hand-dyed Wools

(207) 515-0843

www.paintedmermaiddesigns.com
South Paris, Maine

Seven Gables
Visit our New studio at
316 Main Street, Norway, ME
207.739.2664
Connie S. Fletcher
sevengablesrughooking.com

Liberty 14" x 20" $32

Old Friends Woolens

Original Primitives
Rug & Punch Needle Designs

"Let what we love, be what we do."

Cathy Tokheim • 4902 90th Ave., Swea City
IA 50590 • (515) 272-4305
http://www.etsy.com/shop/oldfriendswoolens

COLORAMA WOOL
Vivily Powers
Certified McGown Teacher
36 Fairview Street
Manchester, CT 06040
(860) 643-2341

coloramasw@aol.com
Swatches • Specialty Dying
Custom Color Plans • Private and Group Lessons

SPRUCE TOP RUG HOOKING STUDIO INCORPORATED

255 West Main Street
Mahone Bay
Nova Scotia B0J 2E0

Ph 902 624-9312
Fax 902 624-0632
1 888 (RUG HOOK)
1 888 784-4665

chclark@tallships.ca
www.sprucetoprughookingstudio.com

Seasons of the Heart, 30" x 30", #5- to 9-cut wool on linen. Designed and hooked by Joan Sample, Woodinville, Washington, 2010. ANN C. BOTHWELL

Midnight Clear, 30 1/2" x 38 1/4", #8 1/2- and hand-cut wool on linen with crocheted edge (wool strips). Adapted from the folk art of Lori Brechlin by Spruce Ridge Studios and hooked by Kris Miller, Howell, Michigan, 2011.

Tuhay, 44" x 78", #2- and 3-cut wool on monk's cloth. Pattern by Jane McGown; hooked by Marion Sachs, York, Pennsylvania, 2011. BILL BISHOP

Designs In Wool
Primitive Patterns by Mary Johnson

Supplies...952.406.1330
Hand Dyed Wool...As Is Wool

Flower Basket Trio 18" x 22"

www.designsinwool.com

Martina Lesar
Hooked Rug Studio

16311 Mississauga Road
Caledon, Ontario L7C 1X8
(905) 838-3022
www.martinalesar.com

The Black Sheep Legacy Continues

"My love for rug hooking and what Rhonda and EmmaLou have brought to this art, prompted me to carry on their tradition."
— Elinor Barrett

An extensive selection of primitive patterns based on heirloom rugs and textiles, circa 1800s. Newly released designs by Rhonda Manley now available.

www.blacksheepwooldesigns.com
Columbia, Missouri

L. J. Fibers at The Wooly Red Rug

Original primitive ~ folk art designs
hand-dyed wool
and so much more!

www.woolyredrug.com
4630 Wentworth Avenue
Minneapolis, MN 55419
612-964-1165

Early American Life Directory of Traditional American Crafts 2012

J. Conner Hooked Rugs

From custom design services, to workshops and instruction, materials and kits, as well as our NEWEST wool crafts of Penny Rug Kits and Miniature Punch Needle Kits, you'll find it all!

Rose Border Sheep available as pattern only or complete kit, in Hooked Rug or Miniature Punch.

Janet Conner
P.O. Box 224, Hiram, ME 04041
(207) 625-3325

Visit us online at jconnerhookedrugs.com

GoingGray
Patterns • Rug Hangers • Frames • Caddies

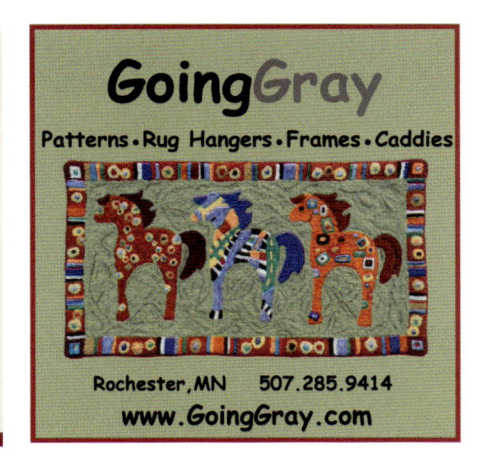

Rochester, MN 507.285.9414
www.GoingGray.com

Hooked Treasures

C-141
Morris Crow
22.5 x 36.5

Cherylyn Brubaker
6 Iroquois Circle • Brunswick, ME 04011
(207) 729-1380 • By Appt. • Catalog $6
www.hookedtreasures.com

The 1840 House
Complete Rug Hooking Supplies
Workshops, Classes, Custom Designing.
Scrolls, Flowers, & Leaves Book—$18.95
Sculptured Rugs in Waldoboro Style—$19.95

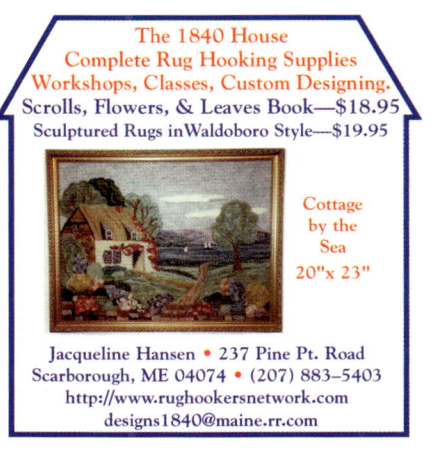

Cottage by the Sea
20"x 23"

Jacqueline Hansen • 237 Pine Pt. Road
Scarborough, ME 04074 • (207) 883-5403
http://www.rughookersnetwork.com
designs1840@maine.rr.com

Finally Finished

Do you LOVE Rug Hooking but...
HATE to finish your pieces?

You're in Luck.
We'll carefully finish them for you.

Call Finally Finished for details:
(603) 526-9265   Ask for Ann

www.RugsFinallyFinished.com
With over 25 years of rug hooking experience.

Woolley Fox

132 Woolley Fox Lane, Ligonier, PA 15658
(724) 238-3004 * www.woolleyfox.com

Purple Peeps

Hooked by Kathy Ashcom
Armagh, PA

Fun to hook!
Great light and bright,
or dark and dirty.
Play with patches of color
in the background.

23 x 36
Monk's Cloth $49.00, Linen $73.00

2012 catalogs are available!
Call, or visit our website to order yours.

The Wool Studio
328 Tulpehocken Ave.
West Reading, PA 19611
Rebecca Erb
phone 610.678.5448
fax 610.750.6326
Quality Imported Woolens

Your "Go-To" Source for Lights!

Luxurious 100% Wool!

Send $5 for wool samples

Shopper-tunity Days Celebration
info @ www.thewoolstudio.com
Contact us via e-mail at
thewoolstudio@comcast.net

WOOD N WOOL
RUG HOOKING STATION

FRAMES
STANDS
HOOKS

(512) 431-0431
www.woodnwool.com

LIZIANA CREATIONS

www.liziana.com

PO Box 310
Shelburne, MA 01370-0310

Open by Appointment

diana@galaxy.net
413 625-9403
mikeandlizob@cox.net
860 289-0430

Catalogue - $6 ppd

Complete Rug Hooking Supplier

American Country Rugs

Lucille B. Festa

East Rupert, Vermont

www.americancountryrugs.com

INDEX TO ADVERTISERS

American Country Rugs	128
Ault's Rug Hooking Store	110
Bee Line-Townsend Cutters	Inside Back Cover
Black Sheep Wool	127
Cambria Pines Rug Camp, Inc.	110
Colorama Wool	125
Designs in Wool	127
Dorr Mill Store	Back Cover
Finally Finished	127
Fluff & Peachy Bean	133
Goat Hill Designs	133
Going Gray	127
Green Mountain Hooked Rugs, Inc.	125
Gruber's	110
Halcyon Yarn	56
Harry Fraser	135
Hooked in the Mountains Rug Show	110
Hooked Treasures	127
Howard Brush	135
J. Conner	127
Jacqueline Hansen, The 1840 House	127
L.J. Fibers	127
Little House Rugs	135
Liziana Creations	128
Martina Lesar	127
Merry Hooker Woolens	135
Old Friends Woolens	125
Painted Mermaid Designs	125
RHM Marketplace	120
Pine Island Primitives	133
Ruckman Mill Farm	125
Sauder Village	5
Searsport Rug Hooking	6
Seaside Rug Hooking	133
Seven Gables Rug Hooking	125
Spruce Ridge Studios	125
Spruce Top Rug Hooking Studio	125
With Hook in Hand	133
The Wool Studio	128
The Woolery	84
W. Cushing & Company	Inside Front Cover
Woolley Fox	128
Wood N Wool	128

Dear Celebration Reader:

Which rugs are your favorites?

The judges have chosen the finalists—now it is up to you to tell us which of these rugs deserves the honor of being named Readers' Choice winners.

Review each of the winning rugs carefully and make your selections—1st, 2nd, and 3rd choice for each of the Commercial, Original, Adaptation, and Primitive categories. Mark your choices on the attached ballot and be sure to mail it in before December 31, 2012.

Or vote online. Go to *www.rughookingmagazine.com*, and look for the *Celebration* Readers' Choice link.

RHM appreciates the time you take to send in your Readers' Choice vote. Please help us honor the rug hooking artists represented within the pages of *Celebration XXII* by voting for your choice of the best of the best.

Sincerely,

Debra Smith

Editor

TEAR OFF HERE

READERS' CHOICE BALLOT

After reviewing all the rugs, fill out this ballot and mail it in to vote (Canadians, please use an envelope and your own postage). The winners of the Readers' Choice Contest will be announced in the June/July/August 2013 issue of *Rug Hooking* magazine. **Note: Ballots must be received by December 31, 2012.**

ORIGINAL RUG
- 1ST CHOICE
- 2ND CHOICE
- 3RD CHOICE

ADAPTATIONS
- 1ST CHOICE
- 2ND CHOICE
- 3RD CHOICE

COMMERCIAL RUG
- 1ST CHOICE
- 2ND CHOICE
- 3RD CHOICE

PRIMITIVE
- 1ST CHOICE
- 2ND CHOICE
- 3RD CHOICE

NAME
ADDRESS
CITY/STATE/ZIP   PHONE NUMBER

Never miss an edition of
CELEBRATION OF HAND-HOOKED RUGS
by joining our Automatic Shipment Program

Yes! I want to make sure I never miss an edition of *Celebration of Hand-Hooked Rugs*. Please sign me up for your risk-free automatic shipment program. I understand each time a new **Rug Hooking** book is published it will be automatically shipped to me; this includes our annual edition of *Celebration of Hand-Hooked Rugs*. Each book will be mine to examine for 21 days. If I like what I see, I'll keep the book and pay the invoice. If I'm not delighted, I'll return the book at *Rug Hooking* magazine's expense, and owe nothing.

NAME
ADDRESS
CITY/STATE/ZIP   PHONE NUMBER
E-mail Address

BCEL12

SUBSCRIBE TODAY!
RUG HOOKING

Subscribe today and let us make you a better rug hooker

☐ **YES!** Sign Me Up Now.
Send me 5 issues of *Rug Hooking* magazine for just $34.95*—that's more than 34% off the newsstand cover price.

☐ I prefer 2 years (10 issues), for just $62.95.
☐ Payment enclosed
☐ Bill me later
For credit card payment call
1 (877) 462-2604

Name
Address
City
State   Zip
May we e-mail you about your subscription? ☐ Yes ☐ No
E-mail Address

* Canadian please add $5 per year for shipping and handling, plus taxes. Please allow 6-8 weeks for your first issue to arrive.

BCEL12

PLACE
STAMP
HERE

RUG HOOKING MAGAZINE
5067 Ritter Rd.
Mechanicsburg, PA 17055-6921

PLACE
STAMP
HERE

Subscription Department
351 Riverside Industrial Parkway
Portland, ME 04103-1415

NO POSTAGE
NECESSARY
IF MAILED
IN THE
UNITED STATES

BUSINESS REPLY MAIL
FIRST-CLASS MAIL PERMIT NO. 22 PORTLAND ME

POSTAGE WILL BE PAID BY ADDRESSEE

Subscription Department
351 Riverside Industrial Parkway
Portland, ME 04103-1415

Celebrating PRIMITIVE DESIGN

Antique Heart in Hand Redux, 36" x 60", #6- and 8-cut wool on linen.
Adapted from an antique rug and hooked by Norma Batastini, Glen Ridge, New Jersey, 2010. BILL BISHOP

Primitive rugs are one of the most beloved and traditional styles of rug hooking. This is the first year that *Celebration* has included a distinct primitive category, so we decided to show you a few more of the entries. Though these gems did not make the finalist listing as chosen by the judges, they are fine examples of primitive rug hooking at its best.

Elaine's Antique Runner, 31" x 57", #8½-cut wool on linen. Pattern by Woolley Fox; hooked by Debra Inglis, San Augustine, Texas, 2011. WENDY FLOYD

Unbridled, 22" x 30", #6-cut wool on linen.
Pattern by Charco by Robin Price; hooked by Susan Higgins, San Francisco, California, 2011.

Oliver Cromwell, 31½" x 42½", #7-cut wool on linen. Designed and hooked by Cora Maldonado, Texas City, Texas, 2011. BELINDA CANALES/MEMORIES IN PICTURES

Peace, Love and Dan, 47" x 36½", #8-cut as-is and hand-dyed wool on linen.
Designed and hooked by Laurie Wiles, Edmonton, Alberta, Canada, 2011.

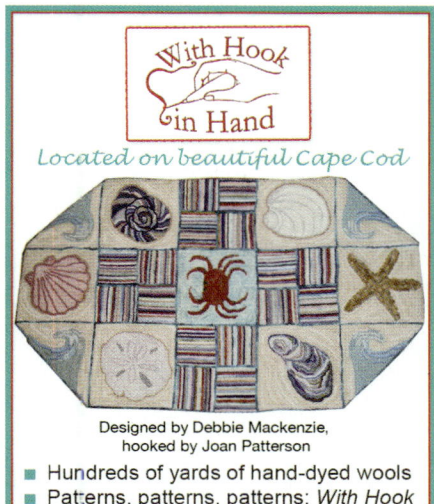

With Hook in Hand
Located on beautiful Cape Cod

Designed by Debbie Mackenzie, hooked by Joan Patterson

- Hundreds of yards of hand-dyed wools
- Patterns, patterns, patterns: *With Hook in Hand* collection and other designers
- Pre-cut Kits and Color-planning
- Beeline-Townsend Cutters
- Frames, Hooks and more
- Weekly classes and Monthly Hookins

"We're A Gathering Place for Wool Lovers"

Open Monday-Saturday 10-4
We have moved!
1368 Rte. 134, PO Box 1015
East Dennis, MA 02641
508-385-HOOK (4665)
www.withhookinhand.com
Norma McElhenny—Owner

Gail Dufresne's Goat Hill Designs

- Original designs
- Kits and patterns
- A huge selection of wools
- Ritchie, Hartman & Miller hooks and many others
- Visit me online or make an appointment to visit me
- And so much more

Custom dyeing is my specialty. There's nothing I can't dye!

Check out our NEW website@ Goathilldesigns.com

Visit me online Or call 609-397-4885

PINE ISLAND primitives

Olde Flag 16" x 23" or 29" x 43"

Workshops at the Farm
September 12–14, 2012
November 5–7, 2012
January 16–18, 2013

Sally Kallin
Patterns • Wool • Workshops
Color Catalog $12

16369 County 11 Blvd.
Pine Island, MN 55963
(507) 356-2908
e-mail: rugs@pitel.net

www.pineislandprimitives.com

Fluff & Peachy Bean Designs
Whimsical Designs for Rug Hooking
Glorious Hand Dyed Wool

"Snuggled In"
10in. x 18in.

Pattern on Linen..$30.00
*plus shipping

Wool (only) $125.00
*plus shipping

www.fluffpeachybeandesigns.com

Seaside Rug Hooking Company

Color Catalog or OnLine
Rughookseaside.com

Patterns for Everyone

Celebration XXII 2012 • 133

Shippee Floral, 64" x 32", #6-, 8½-, 9½-, and hand-cut wool on linen. Pattern by Woolley Fox; hooked by Weslee Hursh, Brownsville, Pennsylvania, 2011.

Newfoundland Lion, 43½" x 28", #6- to 9-cut wool on monk's cloth. Adapted from an antique rug and hooked by Pam Upton, Lake Crystal, Minnesota, 2010.

FRASER Rug Making Equipment

Bliss Model A

Fraser 500-1

Complete Rug Hooking and Braiding Supplies

HARRY FRASER COMPANY
R & R MACHINE CO. INC.
498 Trot Valley Road
Stuart, Virginia 24171
(276) 694-5824
www.fraserrug.com

Fraser Keepsake Pattern catalog,
includes patterns $20
Pat Hornafius, Karlkraft, Heritage Hill

E-mail: fraserrugs@gmail.com

The Merry Hooker Woolens

The Finest Hand Dyed Woolens
Beautiful Plaid & Textured Woolens
Patterns, Kits & Dyeing Supplies
Workshops & Classes

Featuring...
Beeline-Townsend
Fabric Cutters

Call (925) 980-9463 or visit our website at:
www.TheMerryHookerWoolens.com

---

joy with yarn! OF HOOKING
by Judy Taylor

The long awaited sequel to "Hooking with Yarn" features some 300 yarn-hooked rugs, including the work of yarn-hookers from all over North America. Also included is an award-winning DVD and 4 full-size patterns.

"Easier than hooking with wool strips and lots more fun too!"
K. MacPhail, Bellevue, WA

"Beyond terrific, informative, easy to understand, clear and precise." V. Ellenwood, Orland, FL

To order, please visit
www.littlehouserugs.com

Howard Brush
RENOWNED SINCE 1866

The Original **Rug Hooking Kits & Gripper Strips** Made in USA

All of our products are handcrafted in Woonsocket, Rhode Island. We manufacture rug hooking strips that are great for wall hangings and tapestries. These allow you to hang your fabric art with no lacing or tacking required so you won't damage it. These strips are also perfect for rug hooking frames which grip the rug backing allowing the pattern to be repositioned in seconds. Our goal is to offer quality hand card tools and drum carding cloth at a reasonable price to keep the craft of spinning affordable. By doing so we are quickly becoming the supplier of choice for the fiberarts community.

NEW! We are proud to introduce our newest rug hooking Channel Frame kit! This kit incorporates wood channels into which you can easily slide your rug hooking strips an remove them from the channel with ease. Available in kit form as shown, they are perfect for any project where you would need to change strips frequently, or need your strips secured properly without use of adhesives or staples. Thus, one frame can suit multiple backings.

Call or check our website for a dealer near you!

800-556-7710
www.howardbrush.com/rughook.html

Remember, 36" x 24", #6- and 8-cut wool on linen. Inspired by limestone carvings over the door of the Alamo (1715) and hooked by Georgeanne Wertheim, San Antonio, Texas, 2011. RON TRAVIS

Shenandoah Valley Eagle, 63" x 24", #8½-cut wool on linen.
Pattern by Woolley Fox/Barbara Carroll; hooked by Crystal Brown, Washington, Pennsylvania, 2011.